Flies for Saltwater

BY DICK STEWART & FARROW ALLEN

Book Design and Illustrations • Larry Largay
Photography • Dick Stewart

Published by Mountain Pond Publishing
P.O. Box 797
North Conway, NH 03860
USA

Distributed by Lyons & Burford
31 West 21 Street
New York, NY 10010
USA

Printed in the United States of America by Capital Offset Company

Third Printing

Library of Congress
        Stewart, Dick.
            Flies for Saltwater / by Dick Stewart & Farrow Allen ; book
        design and illustrations, Larry Largay; photography, Dick
        Stewart — 1st ed. — Intervale, NH, USA : Mountain Pond
        Publishing ; New York, NY, USA : Distributed by Lyons &
        Burford, c1992.
                vii, 80, [7] p. : col. ill. ; 29 cm. — (Fishing flies of North America ; 4th)
                Includes bibliographical references (p [83]) and index.
                ISBN 0-936644-12-5 (hardcover). — ISBN 0-936644-13-3 (softcover)

            1. Flies, Artificial—North America.   2. Saltwater fly fishing—North
        America.   3. Fly tying.   I. Allen, Farrow. II. Title. III. Series.
        SH451.S7175 1992   688.7'912—dc20   93-237947
                                                    AACR 2   MARC

PREFACE

Beginning around the mid 1800s, books about trout and salmon flies became commonplace. Today, hundreds of such titles are available for the devoted fly fishermen and each year a dozen or so new titles are added to the list. For the saltwater enthusiast, however, there is a paucity of books devoted to saltwater flies and only three such books have ever been published, all within the past twenty years. Interestingly, an explosion of interest in saltwater fly fishing has resulted in a corresponding proliferation in the quantity and variety of flies designed for saltwater's specific challenges. This book attempts to document those flies which have proved to be successful in catching saltwater gamefish, and to introduce the new flies and fly tying techniques which significantly expand the options available to the modern angler.

The 1980s and early 1990s have been witness to an unprecedented growth of interest in fly fishing in saltwater. And, this expansion has not just been in the traditional areas such as inshore fly fishing. A combination of circumstances has made coastal waters the new destination for recreational fly fishing. Improved, affordable air travel and increased discretionary leisure time have provided the opportunity for growing numbers of anglers to travel. In many parts of the country increased angling pressures have resulted in reduced angling success in freshwater lakes and streams. This decline has motivated many dedicated fly fishers to seek new angling destinations; and where better than the still (somewhat) unexplored saltwaters where the opportunity to catch big fish always exists.

Up until less than twenty years ago the average fly fisherman had to overcome numerous obstacles in order to fly fish in the salt, and it was only a handful of anglers who pioneered the sport. Much of what we know today is the direct result of the efforts of these early flyrodders. The true pioneers, such as Henshall, Loving, Dimock, Rhode and Gibbs, had to overcome many limitations of both travel and equipment, but they persisted and established a foundation to be used by others. Later came anglers and writers who have helped bring saltwater fly fishing from infancy to maturity - and they have done this in a span of just the past fifty years. Paving the way for all to follow were Joe Brooks and Al McClane, closely followed by Stu Apte, Dan Blanton, Chico Fernandez, Lefty Kreh, Billy Pate, Mark Sosin and Lou Tabory. These are the personalities whose names are familiar to fly fishing devotees, but all of them would agree that any credit should be shared with the many unnamed anglers and guides whose experiences and observations provided much new knowledge. Recent years have produced yet another crop of writers, guides and video personalities who are quickly expanding the frontiers of saltwater flyrodding.

Those of us who fished saltwater some twenty or more years ago have been blessed by the improvements in equipment since that time. We remember heavy nine-foot, metal-ferruled, fiberglass rods, and the only commonly available reels which were simply large-capacity, freshwater models, that often corroded and froze up despite our best preventative efforts. By comparison, modern saltwater fly fishing equipment is simply a pleasure to use. Many of the latest generation of graphite fly rods are designed specifically for saltwater use. They are lightweight, easy to cast, yet strong enough to handle very large fish. Quite a contrast to a few years ago. Reels, too, have improved immensely, with numerous models available featuring large line capacities and strong drag systems that will subdue very large gamefish, including blue marlin. New specialized fly lines complete the selection of basic equipment which has benefited from modern technology - and which has made fly fishing in big water a much more pleasant experience.

The flies used in saltwater have also undergone a major transformation. Because saltwater fly fishing has such a short history, very few flies have had the opportunity to be called "old standards," a term with which most freshwater fly fishers are familiar. In fact, it is unusual to find many of the older fly patterns being offered for sale by the modern fly fishing shop. In the course of researching material for this book it became apparent that the foremost criterion of a saltwater fly is its effectiveness while being fished. This contrasts with some of the Atlantic salmon, steelhead, trout and bass flies which, for artistic appeal, are often tied with exotic materials. Not being tradition bound, saltwater fly tiers have been receptive to experimenting with synthetic materials, some of which were never intended for fly tying, and with the newer glues and adhesives. One needs only to look at the epoxy flies, or some of the crab and shrimp patterns, to see how imaginative fly tiers are contributing to their craft.

We encountered a bit of resistance from a few guides who were a little reluctant to share all of their "secret flies," since their livelihood is tied to reputations for success. While we understand their concerns, it makes us appreciate all the more those contributors to this book who were so willing to share their knowledge and ideas with their fellow fly tiers.

Any reference of this sort requires that we attempt to classify and categorize all of the flies. We wrestled with several classification methods before deciding on the one selected, and in some instances the demarcation between fly styles may not be fully evident. In the absence of any established standard we hope you will find this a reasonable and useful presentation.

The emphasis of this book is on presenting a combination of proven, successful fly designs together with some of the very newest ideas in saltwater fly tying. Some flies are simple, others are complex, but all serve the angler well - they catch fish. We have not specified the sizes in which to tie these flies, although for some of the larger flies we have stated the length of the fly we photographed so that you might have a point of reference. We have also avoided the specific references to the brand names of hooks or materials because we believe that these matters are best left to the discretion of the individual fly tier.

Because of the cooperation of everyone who generously contributed flies for this book, we believe that it is the most up-to-date, complete, and useful reference ever published about saltwater flies. We would like to emphasize that it is the direct result of the participation of the many guides and fly tiers whose flies appear within. This is their book; these are their ideas; we have served primarily as compilers with the desire to select, organize and present the ideas and products of the many anglers who were willing to share their experience and knowledge. Our thanks, foremost, is to these fly tiers.

We would like to add one last note of appreciation. A long time friend, Fran Stuart, was actively helping in the proofreading of this book when she unexpectedly passed away. Fran always inspired and urged us to do our best - less than that was not sufficient. She was an enthusiastic fly tier and a great supporter. We'll miss her.

CONTENTS

Tarpon Streamers

APTE TARPON FLY, ORIGINAL

Wing: A pair of bright red-orange hackles outside of which are a pair or two of bright yellow hackles, curving out, tied over the hook point
Collar: Two yellow and two red-orange hackles wound together
Head: Red-orange with a coat of clear epoxy

This 1969 tarpon pattern was one of the first to place the wing at the rear.

APTE TOO, ORIGINAL

Wing: Four to eight furnace hackles outside of which is sparse pearlescent crystal flash; a mono loop tail support under all
Collar: Gray squirrel tail
Head: Red, with painted white eyes with black pupils

Finding large flies unnecessary, Apte pioneered the use of small tarpon flies.

APTE TOO PLUS, BLACK DEATH

Wing support: A loop of monofilament extending from the rear of the hook shank
Wing: Black rabbit fur strip and a few strands of pearl crystal flash
Collar: Gray squirrel tail dyed red
Head: Fluorescent red, eyes optional

APTE TOO PLUS, ORIGINAL

Wing support: A loop of monofilament extending from the rear of the hook shank
Wing: Rusty brown rabbit fur strip and a few strands of pearl crystal flash
Collar: Natural red squirrel tail
Head: Burnt orange, with white eyes with black pupils

BLACK DEATH

Wing: Two bright red hackles flanked by four to six black hackles
Collar: Red hackle
Head: Fluorescent red

There are many variations of this popular Florida Keys style tarpon fly. In the Keys nearly any tarpon streamer constructed with a combination of red and black feathers or hair is called a Black Death.

BLACK DEATH MARABOU

Wing: Three pairs of black hackles curving out over which are strands of red crystal flash
Collar: Red marabou
Head: Red thread coated with epoxy

The Black Death is often dressed for tarpon with a wing of red bucktail and black hackle, and a red hackle collar.

Tied by Jack Gartside

Tied by Florida Keys Outfitters

BLUE SUNSET

Wing: Fluorescent orange hackle outside of which is grizzly hackle dyed yellow
Collar: Raccoon body fur dyed kingfisher blue
Head: Fluorescent red, with yellow eyes with black pupils

Jack Gartside particularly likes this fly for dirty water or dark overcast days.

BROWN/ORANGE/GRIZZLY

Wing: Pearl Flashabou over which, on each side, are sets of one grizzly hackle dyed orange and two grizzly hackles dyed brown, curving out
Collar: Grizzly hackles dyed brown and grizzly hackles dyed orange, mixed
Head: Fluorescent red thread, coated with epoxy

This is one of the most productive color combinations for tarpon.

Tied by Dick Stewart

Tied by Jon Cave

CASA MAR SPECIAL

Wing: Red bucktail outside of which are several wide white hackles over which is pearl Flashabou
Collar: Hot orange calftail
Head: Silver bead chain eyes with red thread

This fly was developed by Bill Barnes for Rio Colorado tarpon in Costa Rica.

CAVE'S TARPON RATTLER

Wing: 6 to 8 strands of pearl crystal flash, on each side of which are 2 or 3 red dyed grizzly hackles and a natural grizzly hackle curving out
Underbody: Glass, metal or plastic worm rattle, secured to the hook shank
Collar: Gray squirrel tail dyed red
Head: Red thread covering over the rattle chamber, epoxy coated

Tied by Dick Stewart

Tied by Dick Stewart

CHINESE CLAW

Wing: Two bright yellow hackles curving in with two grizzly hackles on each side curving out
Collar: Grizzly or black and grizzly hackles mixed
Head: Black, epoxy coated

Over the years this classic tarpon fly has accounted for many big fish.

COCKROACH

Wing: Four to eight grizzly hackles
Collar: Natural brown bucktail, gray or red squirrel tail
Head: Black

Lefty Kreh in his book *Salt Water Fly Patterns* describes the Cockroach as a "Deceiver fly first tied by John Emery." Tied with several different collars, the Cockroach tied in this deceiver style is popular for tarpon in clear water.

Tarpon Streamers

COCKROACH, CHICO'S

Wing: Four to eight grizzly hackles curving out
Collar: Black bear hair
Head: Black
This Chico Fernandez variation of the Cockroach is dressed in the familiar "Keys style," with the wing and collar above the hook point.

ESTAZ COLLAR TARPON FLY

Wing: Splayed, a fluorescent yellow hackle between two black hackles
Hackle: Two fluorescent yellow and two fluorescent blue, mixed
Collar: Black pearlescent Estaz chenille
Head: Black thread, tapered as shown, overwrapped with pearlescent black crystal flash and finished with a fluorescent red tip

HOMOSASSA DECEIVER

Wing #1:   Hot orange badger hackles with a yellow hackle skirt
Sides: Short grizzly hackle dyed hot orange, orange calftail over, yellow calftail collaring sides
Wing #2:   Black and pearlescent crystal flash over which is peacock herl
Collar: White calftail below, orange calftail above

HOMOSASSA SPECIAL

Tail: Four yellow dyed grizzly hackles
Wing: Four yellow dyed grizzly hackles, evenly spaced along the hook shank length
Collar: Yellow bucktail striped with a black marking pen
Head: Orange with white eyes with black pupils

KIME'S RED & BLACK TARPON FLY

Tail: Sparse blue crystal flash or Flashabou outside of which are eight or more black hackles curving out
Body: Gray and black variegated chenille
Collar: Red calftail
Eyes: Large silver bead chain secured with red thread

MICROJET 'POON ACCELER-ATOR

Tail: Black Twinkle, or black crystal flash
Butt: Burnt orange sparkle chenille
Wing: Two grizzly hackles curving out; skirt of brown rabbit fur
Shoulder: Sharptail grouse body feather
Collar: Black rabbit fur strip, palmered
Head: Fluorescent red

MOORE'S PINK TARPON

Wing:	Narrow grizzly, narrow black, wide bright pink (cerise) and narrow grizzly hackles on each side curving outward
Collar:	Bright pink (cerise) hackle, heavy
Head:	Fluorescent rose thread, covered with epoxy

Winston Moore has tarpon fished for over 30 years and this fly is his favorite.

MOORE'S YELLOW AND GRIZZLY

Wing:	3 pairs of bright yellow hackles flanked on each side by a small grizzly hackle
Collar:	Red hackle tied dry fly style
Head:	Red or fluorescent orange

ORANGE BUTT TARPON

Wing:	Light tan wool over which is a pair of furnace and a pair of grizzly hackles curving in, and orange crystal flash over all
Body:	Fluorescent pink-orange chenille
Collar:	Gray fox guard hairs
Head:	Cream

ORANGE GRIZZLY TARPON FLY

Wing:	Orange crystal flash over which are six dyed orange grizzly hackles with cheeks of orange dyed guinea body feathers, all curving out
Collar:	Hot orange
Head:	Fluorescent orange

Jimmy Nix likes to call this one his "meat and potatoes tarpon fly."

POON WALKER

Wing:	Short bunch of orange calftail outside of which are 6 blue hackles curving out, and sparse pearl crystal flash. Make a wrap of orange chenille around the base of the wing to prevent fouling.
Collar:	Orange calftail
Head:	Fluorescent orange with painted yellow eyes with black pupils, coated with epoxy

PURPLE FUZZY TARPON

Wing:	Purple calftail outside of which are 6 purple hackles curving out, and purple crystal flash
Collar:	Purple calftail
Head:	A wrap of fluorescent rose chenille around the base of the collar; the rest of the head is purple chenille

Tarpon Streamers

Tied by Jon Olch

RABBIT WIGGLE BOMBER

Tail: White chamois, leather or latex, cut in a "U" shape as shown
Body: Lead wire underbody and black sparkle chenille or standard black chenille ribbed with fine silver Mylar
Collar: Pearl Flashabou, a turn of white marabou, a turn of red rabbit fur
Eyes: Silver bead chain on top secured with fluorescent orange thread

Tied by Dick Stewart

RED AND WHITE TARPON FLY

Wing: Three or four white hackles on each side curving out
Collar: Red hackle
Head: Fluorescent red
In his book *Salt Water Fly Patterns*, Lefty Kreh refers to this fly as "perhaps the best all-around fly ever developed for tarpon."

Tied by Dick Stewart

RHODE'S TARPON STREAMER

Wing: Six to ten long white hackles, curving out
Collar: Red hackle wrapped dry fly style over red thread
Head: Red
Homer Rhodes, Jr., of Miami, was a pioneer of saltwater fly fishing and his Tarpon Streamer served as a prototype for many modern designs.

Tied by Farrow Allen

ROB'S TARPON FLY

Wing: Two furnace hackles curving in and cemented together at the tips
Skirt: Natural badger hair with about half of the underfur removed
Sides: Strands of orange crystal flash on each side, to the end of the skirt
Collar: Several turns of hot orange hackle (optional)
Head: Fluorescent orange

Tied by Mike Wolverton

SEA BUNNY, RUST

Tail support (optional): Loop of stiff monofilament or a tuft of stiff hair
Tail: Rust colored rabbit fur strip over orange pearlescent crystal flash
Collar: Cross-cut rust colored rabbit fur strip, wrapped
Head: Fluorescent orange with yellow eyes with black pupils
The original "Bunny" was tied in rust color and did not contain any crystal flash. Tarpon Bunnies are tied in a wide range of colors.

Tied by George Kesel

STEARN'S PINFISH

Wing: White FisHair tied 360 degrees around the hook and striped on the upper portion with a green marking pen. On each side are several strands of pearl crystal flash with peacock herl over
Head: Green with white eyes with black pupils
Bob Stearns originated this pinfish imitation specifically for tarpon.

SUNRISE - SUNSET

Wing: White marabou flanked by 2 white hackles outside of which are two fluorescent green hackles and pearl Flashabou
Collar: Fluorescent green over white Fish Fuzz or similar
Head: Fluorescent green with painted fluorescent red eyes with black pupils

TARPON FINGER MULLET

Tag and body: Fluorescent red tying thread
Wing: White bucktail over which are four to six white hackles with pearl crystal flash on the sides. Above and in front are more strands of crystal flash, peacock herl and a single grizzly hackle on each side
Collar: Grizzly hackle, silver bead chain eyes with gray chenille around

TARPON GLO, BAD CRAB

Wing: Red squirrel tail flanked on each side by four orange and four light furnace hackles, curving out
Cheeks: A gold, black tipped, cock ringneck pheasant shoulder feather
Collar: Orange hackle or red-orange cock pheasant body feather
Head: Burnt orange with painted yellow eyes with black pupils

TARPON GLO, ORANGE

Wing: Brown bucktail or red squirrel, on each side is a grizzly hackle dyed red between two natural grizzly hackles, curving out
Collar: Grizzly hackles, mixed natural and dyed red
Head: Fluorescent green and orange, as shown
Eyes: Painted black with white pupils

TARPON MUDDLER

Tail: Large bunch of orange marabou over which is pearl crystal flash and a small bunch of brown marabou
Body: Brown yarn
Wing: Sparse pearl crystal flash
Collar and head: Natural deer body hair, spun and clipped muddler style
Eyes: Silver bead chain
Developed by Sandy Moret, the school director at the Florida Keys Fly Fishing School & Outfitters in Islamorada, Florida.

WHITE LIGHTNING

Wing: A few strands of pearl Flashabou over which is a set of two white hackles, outside of which is a grizzly hackle dyed chartreuse and a white hackle curving outward on each side
Collar: Yellow marabou
Head: Fluorescent green thread, coated with epoxy
Originated by Steve Huff, a guide as well as an instructor at the Florida Keys Fly Fishing School & Outfitters in Islamorada.

Crabs

Tied by Bill Catherwood

Tied by Tim Borski

Tied by Joe Blados

Tied by Del Brown

ARTICULATED CRAB

Hook: Straight eye, short shank
Hook dressing: Sand cemented to a base of built up thread and wire
Connection: Wire loops connect the hook to a wire, cross-shaped frame on which the fly is constructed
Eyes: Melted monofilament beads, black
Claws: Two brown and black mottled body feathers with heavy curved stems, cemented into shape with the barbs all pulled forward
Legs: Ginger variant hackles secured to the base of the claws, 4 per side
Back: Speckled brown hen body feather
Underbelly: Speckled brown hen body feather

Bill Catherwood designed this fly to imitate a crab with its claws raised in a defensive position. The sand camouflages the hook and blends with sandy bottoms. There are many crab imitations, but Catherwood's design is surely unique.

CHERNOBYL CRAB

Hook: Straight eye, standard length
Tail (claws): White calftail outside of which is orange crystal flash and two dark furnace hackles curving out
Body: Natural brown deer body hair, spun and clipped flat and crab shaped
Legs: Long, soft tan hackle, palmered and trimmed across the bottom
Eyes: Lead dumbbell eyes, painted yellow with black pupils

Borski says that this is his best mudding bonefish fly. Very effective in late winter when big bonefish can often be found schooling in three to six feet of water.

CREASE FLY CRAB

Hook: Straight eye, long shank
Eyes: Melted monofilament
Legs: Leather strips
Body and legs: A piece of "Livebody" sheet foam rubber, trimmed to shape, including legs or claws, folded over to form the top and bottom, glued together over the hook shank with a heavy duty CA cement and pinched together until fastened
Mouth and feelers: Tip of a hackle, spread out and cemented across the underbody
Note: Paint the body and legs and coat the top and bottom of the shell with epoxy

This is a crab pattern from Joe Blados of Southhold, New York, that can be made in whatever size or color you need.

DEL BROWN'S PERMIT FLY

Hook: Straight eye, standard length
Tail (claws): Sparse pearl Flashabou over which are four to six ginger variant hackle tips curving out
Legs: White rubber hackle with red tips
Body: Alternating strands of tan and brown yarn, tied along the shank using fluorescent green thread
Eyes: Chrome lead dumbbell eyes secured with fluorescent green thread

Del Brown's Permit Fly, formerly known as Del's Merkin, is one of the most popular as well as most productive crab patterns being fished for permit from the Florida Keys southward. It is also effective for bonefish and mutton snapper.

EPOXY CRAB

Hook: Straight eye, standard length
Tail (claws): About four strands of pearl Flashabou over which are two ginger variant hackles curving out

over which is light tan marabou
Eyes: Melted monofilament
Head: Olive-tan epoxy
Weedguard: .019" hard nylon

Sandy Moret of the Florida Keys Fly Fishing School & Outfitters recommends this impressionistic crab pattern for bonefish, permit, redfish and mutton snapper.

Tied by Florida Keys Outfitters

EPOXY DIAMOND CRAB

Hook: Straight eye, standard length
Eyes: Stiff monofilament, melted on each end and tied across the shank
Weight: A flat piece of lead trimmed to a "V" laid on top of the hook and covered with thread
Body: Fine wire or monofilament attached at the bend, pulled forward

over the eyes on each side, secured behind the eye of the hook and filled in with brown tinted epoxy
Wing: Light tan calftail over which is pearl crystal flash and a pair of tan grizzly hackle tips curving in
Note: Best colors are brown, tan, pink and yellow

Joe Branham, a professional fly tier from Valdosta, Georgia, developed this diamond shaped semi-translucent crab primarily for bonefish and redfish. Recently it's acquired a good reputation for permit as well.

Tied by Joe Branham

ERIC'S STANDING CRAB

Hook: Straight eye, standard length, with 6 to 10 lead wire wraps on the bend
Head: Orange crystal flash over which is tan grizzly marabou
Claws: Two matched cree hackles per side, with the tips cut away
Weight: Lead dumbbell tied below hook eye
Legs: Rubber bands or hackle, knotted and spotted with a marking pen

Weedguard: 20 lb. mono in a "V" as shown holds fly in a standing position
Body: Tan fleece, applied like Glo-Bug yarn, distributed over the top of the hook, trimmed flat and crab-like (spotted with a marking pen)
Eyes: Melted monofilament cemented into the fleece
Belly: White fabric paint

Designed by Eric Peterson as a companion to Eric's Standing Shrimp (which see). To imitate a floating crab, Peterson ties a variation without lead and with silicone applied to the body.

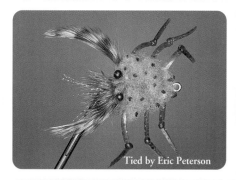

Tied by Eric Peterson

FIDDLER IN THE GRASS

Hook: Straight eye, standard length, with the front ⅓ of the shank bent up slightly
Underbody: Lead wire over the rear ⅓
Body: Brown chenille wrapped over the rear ⅔ of the hook shank
Weedguard: Stiff 20 lb. monofilament, attached in front of the chenille body forming a horizontal oval loop

around the point of the hook, extending a little beyond the bend
Wing: Sparse brown marabou barbs, over which are a few strands of orange crystal flash with a back of two dyed brown grizzly hen hackles tied flat over the hook point and weed guard
Note: Usually tied on a size 2 or 4 hook

Tied by John Bottko of Jacksonville, Florida, to imitate a fiddler crab. Fiddlers are abundant in most tidal marshes and inhabit a variety of structure including mangrove roots and sunken debris. Many tend to burrow in sand or mud, but emerge at dusk or during a low tide to forage in the open.

Tied by John Bottko

Crabs

Tied by Phil Chapman

HARE-BALL CRAB

Hook:	Straight eye, standard length		hackle curving out
Head:	Pearlescent copper crystal flash over which is a bunch of rusty orange calftail and a skirt of palmered black rabbit fur	Eyes:	Melted monofilament dipped in epoxy, oversize
		Collar:	Red-brown rabbit fur strip, wrapped
Claws:	On each side a brown and a grizzly	Thread:	Fluorescent orange

Phil Chapman says that his Hare-Ball Crab tends to hang suspended in the water because of the heavy dressing. Twitching the line slightly creates a breathing motion that doesn't pull the fly away and drives tarpon wild.

Tied by Phil Chapman

IN-FURRY-ATOR

Hook:	Straight eye, standard length	Body:	Palmered natural tan rabbit fur strip followed by dyed brown rabbit fur strip palmered after a second set of grizzly tip legs have been applied
Head:	A mixture of brown bucktail, pearlescent orange crystal flash, black Twinkle and a few turns of orange crystal chenille		
Eyes:	Melted monofilament dipped in clear epoxy	Legs:	Grizzly hackle tips
		Weight:	Lead dumbbells, overwrapped with dark orange crystal chenille
Claws:	Grizzly hackle tips		

Phil Chapman developed this unusual looking crab imitation around 1986. It has proven itself to be a very good pattern for redfish. The fly rides with the point up and the eyes serve as a weedguard.

Tied by Harry Kime

HARRY KIME'S YARN CRAB

Hook:	Straight eye, standard length		a grizzly hackle curving out
Butt:	A small ball made of two or three wraps of white chenille	Weight:	Plain lead dumbbell eyes behind the hook eye
Tail (claws):	Sparse white marabou outside of which are two white hackles and	Body:	Tan and brown synthetic yarn
		Legs:	White rubber hackle

A simple yarn crab can be tied in a variety of sizes and colors as desired. Harry Kime is best known for his exploits fishing for tarpon in Costa Rica.

Tied by Ken Krohel

KROHEL'S PERMIT KRAB

Hook:	Straight eye, long shank		wide rubber bands and painted
Weight:	Lead wire wrapped on the bend of the hook and cemented in place	Diving fin:	Clear Mylar
		Shell:	Leather cut to shape, secured over the Mylar diving fin and painted as shown or however you see fit
Underbody:	Hot glue over shaped cork		
Eyes:	Melted monofilament painted black		
		Underbelly:	White hot glue, feathering out to the edges of the leather shell
Legs and claws:	Trimmed to shape from		

Ken Krohel of Indian Rocks Beach, Florida, developed this fly for his father who had watched a permit chasing a crab and asked his son to imitate it. Krohel, who has caught nearly 40 permit on this pattern, says it "sinks and lands with its claws up." When retrieved it swims vertically to the surface and sinks back so a permit gets another chance to eat it.

McCRAB

Hook:	Straight eye, standard length		and the eyes)
Claws:	Pale tan marabou, pearl Flashabou and two brown or ginger variant hackle tips curving out	Eyes:	Burned monofilament
		Legs:	Knotted rubber bands, curving up towards the hook point
Weight:	Lead dumbbells behind hook eye	Weight:	Flat pancake of lead putty, secured on bottom with super glue and covered with white liquid rubber
Body:	Tan elk body hair, spun and clipped flat on the bottom and rounded on top (the bottom hair is saturated with Pliobond for securing the legs		
		Note:	Body and legs are speckled with marine enamel paint

This fly was designed for permit by George Anderson of the Yellowstone Angler, and developed with help from John Barr and Jim Brungardt.

Tied by George Anderson

MONTAGUE'S RATTLE CRAB

Hook:	Straight eye, standard length		ber and a pancake of lead putty to the underside
Eyes:	Stainless steel dressmaker pins		
Claws:	Two ringneck pheasant body feathers curving outward	Legs:	Chamois strips
		Body:	Epoxy applied in two steps, painted opaque dark brown on top and light tan on the bottom (see Montague's Epoxy Permit)
Underbody:	Spun dark deer body hair, trimmed flat like a crab leaving a sizable unclipped bunch around the pincers. Secure a rattle cham-		

The Rattle Crab is successfully fished to tarpon and cobia in large sizes up to 2/0, and to redfish and bonefish in smaller sizes. The rattle chamber reproduces the rattling sound of a crab's legs when scurrying in retreat.

Tied by Jack Montague

NIX'S CRAB

Hook:	Straight eye, standard length	Legs:	Gray rubber hackle
Underbody:	Lead wire	Body:	Several palmered sandy dun hackles, trimmed top and bottom. Over this is a back of four cock ringneck pheasant body feathers, tied flat
Head:	Deer body hair (a short bunch of flared hair helps separate the claws)		
Claws:	Short grizzly hen hackles		
Eyes:	Melted monofilament		

Jimmy Nix developed his crab imitation for redfish off the Gulf Coast of Texas. Nix patterned it after Lew Jewett's Blue Crab and added rubber legs to give the fly more action. It's often tied with a monofilament weed guard as shown.

Tied by Dick Stewart

OLSON CRAB

Hook:	Straight eye, standard length, tied hook point up		shank, giving a mottled appearance, trimmed flat and crab-like
Eyes:	Silver or brass bead chain, secured on top behind the hook eye	Legs:	Bucktail, divided leaving a short "cape" over the top, formed from the butt ends of the bucktail
Tail (claws):	Green and white bucktail, divided		
Body:	Mixed shades of green GloBug yarn tied on underside of the hook	Note:	The above pattern was tied specifically for permit. For bonefish the fly is dressed more sparsely.

The inspiration for this easily constructed crab imitation came from Marty Olson's early experiments tying GloBug yarn egg flies for steelhead and salmon. Olson ties his crab in a wide range of colors, and suggests that red and white, or maroon have worked best for him.

Tied by Marty Olson

Crabs

Tied by Jack Samson

Tied by Redding Fly Shop

Tied by Carl Richards

Tied by Carl Richards

PINK PERMIT CRAB

Hook:	Straight eye, standard length		flattened into the shape of a crab
Weight:	Lead dumbbell eyes	Legs:	Clear Larva Lace knotted with
Claw:	One brown hackle tip over which		strand of pearl crystal flash inside
	is a grizzly hackle tip, both with the	Note:	Legs are secured to the bottom of
	center cut away		the body in a pancake of neutral
Body:	Dubbed pink wool, trimmed and		hot glue.

Jack Samson designed this fly for those days on the flats "... when I can't get a permit to take the McCrab (which see) or a white fly." For him, the Pink Crab has often been the solution.

RAG HEAD CRAB

Hook:	Straight eye, standard length	Body:	Strands of tan yarn, tied along the
Tail (claws):	Sparse pale tan marabou out-		shank, combed out and saturated
	side of which are two pairs of fur-		with cement and covered over with
	nace hackles curving out and olive		loose combed out fibers of yarn
	crystal flash on top		that are liberally sprinkled on. The
Legs:	White round rubber hackle		body should then be squeezed flat
Eyes:	Lead dumbbell eyes secured with		and trimmed round crab-like
	fluorescent green thread		

Designed by Jan Isley, a well known skinny water guide from the Keys to Belize. The Rag Head is considered by many to be one of the best new permit flies of the 1990s.

RICHARDS' IMMATURE BLUE CRAB

Hook:	Straight eye, standard length	Legs and claws:	See below
Eyes:	Melted monofilament painted	Weight:	Flattened lead putty placed to-
	green with black pupils		wards the back on the underside to
Feelers:	Clear monofilament		make the fly sink upright with the
Body:	Cream bug yarn spun on the top of		claws facing upward
	the hook and trimmed to shape	Underside:	White plastic putty

Carl Richards, already well known to the trout fishing community for his books, including *Selective Trout*, has turned his attention to the development of saltwater flies. To achieve lifelike claws and legs Richards first draws a lifesize outline on paper; he then fills in the outline with liquid latex applied with a syringe. Once dry, he accurately colors the latex with Sharpie markers to match the crab species he wishes to imitate. The body is colored to match.

RICHARDS' SOFT SHELL WHARF CRAB

Hook:	Straight eye, standard length		fine marking pens and glued to the
Eyes:	Epoxy beads on monofilament,		body under the hook (see Richards'
	painted amber with black pupils		Immature Blue Crab above)
Body:	Tan Bug Yarn spun on the top of	Weight:	Lead putty
	the hook and trimmed to shape	Underside:	Tan plastic putty or paint over
Legs and claws:	Liquid latex, colored with		the lead, completing the bottom

When forming the legs and claws, Richards uses Rub-R-Mold brand flexible latex which he applies using a disposable syringe. One must have patience, as the latex takes a long time to cure before it can be colored and cemented to the underside of the fly.

STEWART'S SCRAB

Hook: Straight eye, standard length
Antennae: Four strands of black crystal flash
Claws: Six grizzly hackles dyed brown curving out - well separated
Weight: Chrome lead dumbbell eyes on top of the shank above the barb
Head: Fluorescent pink chenille wrapped around the lead eyes

Legs: Orange deer body hair, trimmed to stick out on the sides
Body: Orange deer body hair, and white deer body hair stacked over gray deer body hair, trimmed flat
Eyes: A black craft bead split in half and cemented to the outside of each lead eye

Stewart says that if the claws are well separated with wraps of thread, they will vibrate subtly as the fly settles. The orientation of this fly is with the hook point up. This half shrimp/half crab pattern settles away from the angler when it sinks, insuring a minimum of slack line.

Tied by Jim Stewart

SWIMMING CRAB

Hook: Straight eye, standard length
Body: Tan wool or egg yarn
Eyes: Melted monofilament, painted black, a few strands of pearl crystal flash over
Legs: Blue rubber hackle, knotted, curving up

Claws: Two pairs of grizzly hackle tips
Belly: Epoxy paste (securing the legs, claws, eyes, and crystal flash) painted white
Weight: Plain lead dumbbell eyes tied behind the hook eye

Joe Branham ties saltwater flies in Valdosta, Georgia. He developed this pattern for bonefish and permit with Randall Kaufmann of Kaufmann's Streamborn Flies. Originally called the Wool Crab, Kaufmann later re-named it the Swimming Crab when he put it into his catalog. The fly sinks well and is easy to cast.

Tied by Joe Branham

TARPON CRAB

Tail (claws): Tan calftail over which is orange crystal flash, outside of which is a grizzly hackle between two furnace hackles on each side, curving out
Eyes: Glass taxidermy eyes, extending

back along the sides of the claws
Body: Natural dark deer body hair, spun and trimmed flat. Darkened with a marking pen on top
Legs: Long soft brown hackle wound through the body, trimmed on top

Tim Borski of Islamorada, Florida, designed the Tarpon Crab mainly for fishing at night around bridge pilings. Although it's a great fly in clear water on a bright day, it is most effective after dark from November through February, when resident tarpon are cruising around lighted piers and bridge abutments looking for crabs. As the tide drops, many crabs are set adrift to become easy prey for these tarpon, which range up to 50 or 60 pounds.

Tied by Tim Borski

WOOL OPTIC CRAB

Hook: Straight eye, standard length
Tail (claws): White or light tan marabou over which is orange crystal flash
Claws: Two furnace hackles, curving out
Eyes: Glass taxidermy, extending to the hook bend
Body: Pieces of white yarn tied across the shank, combed out, trimmed to

shape and darkened on top with an olive marking pen
Legs: White rubber hackle applied along with the body yarn, colored with a waterproof marking pen
Weight: Lead dumbbell eyes behind the hook eye

This is one of Tim Borski's crabs for permit. It sinks well and looks like a crab in the water.

Tied by Tim Borski

Tied by Farrow Allen

ARBONA'S SHRIMP

Hook:	Straight eye, standard length
Wing:	Yellow dyed brown bucktail over which is half as much orange bucktail, a few barbs of pink marabou, and a bright orange grizzly hackle tip on each side curving in
Head:	Black and oversized

This shrimp fly was designed by Fred Arbona who is as comfortable around spring creek trout as he is around tarpon and bonefish. Introduced in the early 1980s, this fly is also known as the F. A. Shrimp.

Tied by Brooks Bouldin

BROOKS' SHRIMP

Hook:	Straight eye, long shank
Antennae:	Brown horse mane
Mouth and forelegs:	Brown marabou barbs, 2 light ginger variant hackles curving out over which is short white deer body hair
Eyes:	Black plastic beads on melted monofilament
Head:	Light tan imitation seal over which 2 turns of brown crystal chenille
Abdomen:	Light tan imitation seal fur teased out for legs
Shellback and tail:	Light tan nylon raffia
Rib:	Tan thread

Brooks Bouldin of the Angler's Edge in Houston, originated this shrimp imitation for redfish. It's designed to be fished slightly below the surface, in that space between the floating weeds and those plants growing up from the bottom.

Tied by Jon Cave

CAVE'S SHRIMP WOBBLER

Hook:	Straight eye, standard length
Antennae and forelegs:	Four strands of gold crystal flash over which is a bunch of gold craft fur or other fine hair
Body:	Braided Flashabou Mylar Minnow Body tubing, tied at the bend of the hook leaving some unravelled to form a collar around the antennae and forelegs. Coat the inside of the Mylar tube with a light coat of epoxy, tie off at the head; flatten and mold into a spoon shape
Eyes:	Bead chain, painted black
Note:	After the eyes are attached, coat the entire body with epoxy.

Jon Cave developed the Wobbler in 1985 ". . . to emulate the swimming action of the hardware fisherman's spoon." Originally intended for redfish, it's proven to be appealing to a variety of saltwater species including snook, bluefish, mackerel, barracuda, and seatrout.

COOK'S CRITTER

Hook:	Straight eye, standard length
Tail:	Unravelled pearlescent Mylar tubing
Eyes:	Silver bead chain
Body:	Fluorescent green chenille
Hackle:	Fluorescent green hackle palmered over the body
Shellback:	Pearlescent green Mylar tubing
Wing:	Fluorescent green calftail
Head:	Dark green

Developed for seatrout in the mid-1980s by Vance Cook of Pensacola Beach, Florida. Cook's Critter is an impressionistic shrimp that can be tied in a variety of colors that are effective on bonefish and redfish, but this green variation is still best for trout.

Tied by Vance Cook

CRAFT FUR SHRIMP

Hook: Straight eye, standard length
Tail: Light tan craft fur hair barred with an olive waterproof marking pen, over which are strands of orange crystal flash
Eyes: Lead dumbbell eyes tied under the hook, painted yellow with black pupils
Body: Gold Mylar tinsel
Hackle: Very soft long brown hackle, palmered forward over the body and trimmed on top

Tied by Tim Borski

"A forward swimming shrimp" that was designed by Tim Borski for bonefish, redfish and snook. The long spey-like hackles develop a lot of movement in the water when the fly is retrieved. When wet, the light tan craft fur and long hackle combine to make this fly appear translucent and shrimp-like.

CRUSTACEAN A.D.

Hook: Straight eye, long shank bent into the shape of a Keel hook
Underbody: A piece of lead wire secured to the top-rear section of the hook
Tail: Red squirrel tail with a few strands of olive Flashabou on each side
Eyes: 50 lb. melted monofilament, black
Body: Fluorescent green chenille, overwrapped with fluorescent green crystal chenille
Body hackle: Grizzly dyed fluorescent green, trimmed on top
Shellback: Pearlescent green Mylar tubing
Rib: Heavy white thread over the carapace and rear ⅔ of the hook
Antennae: 30lb. black monofilament, flattened on the tips
Head: Fluorescent green, built up

Tied by Corbett Davis

Creator Corbett Davis of Gulf Breeze, Florida, says this is an effective fly for fishing in shallow grassy areas. Davis perfers a size 6 and suggests using a Duncan Loop for the best action.

ERIC'S STANDING SHRIMP

Hook: Straight eye, standard length
Mouth and forelegs: Orange crystal flash over which is brown marabou, with several wraps of cree hackle at base
Antennae: 2 strands of peacock crystal flash
Eyes: Black beads or melted monofilament
Weight: Small lead dumbbell eye under the hook
Weedguard: 20 lb. mono in a "V" as shown
Tail: Fine brown bucktail. The tips extend over the mouth; the butts are tied down and flared over the lead eyes
Head and abdomen: Brown dubbing
Shellback: Several strands of orange crystal flash cemented inside a trimmed section of clear Ultra Lace
Rib: Light orange thread

Tied by Eric Peterson

Developed for bonefish by Eric Peterson of the Compleat Angler in Southport, Connecticut, this fly maintains an upright position on the bottom, supported by the weedguard.

ESTAZ SHRIMP

Hook: Straight eye, extra long
Antennae, mouth and forelegs: 2 long and 4 short strands of pearl crystal flash, a small bunch of yellow dyed grizzly hackle barbs, and 2 reddish-brown barbs from a cock ringneck pheasant tail. On each side a yellow dyed grizzly hackle tip, splayed (Note: now tie in the cellophane shellback)
Eyes: Gold plastic beads with black pupils on monofilament
Head: Yellow Estaz chenille, a few turns of grizzly hackle dyed yellow
Abdomen: Yellow Estaz chenille
Shellback: Pearlescent (Glitz & Glow) cellophane
Rib: Monofilament

Tied by Oscar Feliu

This glitzy shrimp imitation really turns heads on grassy bonefish flats. It's originator, Oscar Feliu, says it also works well on redfish and seatrout, or whenever a bright shrimp is needed.

Tied by Dick Stewart

FERNANDEZ'S HONEY SHRIMP

Hook:	Straight eye, standard length		copper Flashabou with a cree hackle
Body:	Olive-brown dubbing		on each side
Wing:	Brown craft fur or similar soft hair	Head:	Black
	outside of which are strands of		

Chico Fernandez's Honey Shrimp is a versatile pattern that imitates many of the light brown to tan colored shrimp so common on the bonefish flats. This is a good beginner's fly, which may be weighted for fishing the deeper flats.

Tied by Jon Olch

FLORIDA SHRIMP

Hook:	Straight eye, standard length	Collar:	Grizzly hackle dyed red
Underbody:	Lead wire	Eyes:	Plastic pearlescent bead chain col-
Body:	Braided silver Mylar tinsel		ored pinkish-red with a marking
Wing:	Pink calf tail outside of which are		pen, secured with red thread
	grizzly hackle tips		

The Florida Shrimp was designed by Jon Olch for fishing to bonefish over turtle grass. Olch also says this pattern "works every time" for neophyte anglers when attracting bonefish with chum.

Tied by Tom Lentz

GRASS SHRIMP

Hook:	Straight eye, standard length	Body:	Pink yarn
Tail:	Pink hackle tip	Legs:	Pink hackle, clipped flush on top
Eyes:	Melted monofilament or mono-		and straight across the bottom
	filament dipped in epoxy, colored	Shellback:	Clear plastic
	black	Rib:	Clear monofilament or similar

This is an effective, though somewhat overshadowed, older shrimp pattern that's a variation of the George Phillips' Western Shrimp. During the 1950s Joe Brooks asked Phillips to tie "some pink shrimp" for Florida and almost instantly this fly became Brooks' "favorite for bonefish."

Tied by John Bottko

INCREDIBLE EDIBLE

Hook:	Straight eye, standard length		flat on top
Eyes:	Melted monofilament, black	Shellback:	Clear Mylar or plastic trimmed to
Antennae:	Pearl crystal flash over which is		match the tapering shape of the
	white bucktail		body, including a pointed beak
Forelegs:	Two grizzly hackles curving out		(rostrum)
	and a single turn of guinea hackle	Rib:	Copper wire securing the shellback
Body:	Pink, long fiber crystal chenille,		in place
	trimmed flat on top	Head:	Pink
Legs:	Palmered grizzly hackle, trimmed		

John Bottko of Jacksonville, Florida, designed this shrimp pattern that is very convincing, yet easy to tie.

LENNY'S TARPON SHRIMP, PALE GREEN

Hook: Standard length, straight eye
Wing: Tan marabou over which is pearl crystal flash. On each side are a light green, a ginger and a cree hackle curving out
Eyes: Fluorescent green plastic beads on heavy monofilament and coated with epoxy
Collar: Ginger hackle
Head: Tan chenille

Tied by Lenny Moffo

Lenny Moffo is convinced that the highly visible fluorescent eyes add something special that many tarpon find hard to pass up. This fly can be tied in any color combination desired.

MONTAGUE'S MYSTERY SHRIMP

Hook: Straight eye, long shank
Eyes: Stainless steel dressmaker pins with black heads, epoxy coated
Head: Brown craft fur, dubbed
Legs: Soft brown hackle palmered over the head, on top of which is the base of a brown hackle with the soft barbs protruding on each side
Note: Brown craft fur is tied in behind the head, one end pulled forward over the head and between the eyes, the other end will later be pulled over the abdomen to form a tail.
Body: Epoxy, applied in two stages (see Montagues's Epoxy Permit)
Shellback: A piece of plastic soda straw trimmed to a point and glued over the head, after the first epoxy coat
Tail: Craft fur from the head pulled over the top of the abdomen. Add a final coat of epoxy over abdomen

Tied by Jack Montague

NIX'S EPOXY BACK SHRIMP

Hook: Straight eye, long shank
Mouth: A loosely dubbed ball of cream Angora fur mixed with sparse red, orange and brown fur, around which is a clump of pinkish tan calftail
Antennae: Orange and brown Ultra Hair on each side plus three strands of pearl crystal flash over the top (wrap a few turns of dubbing before applying the eyes)
Eyes: Orange beads of epoxy on mono
Head and abdomen: White Angora mixed with sparse red, orange and brown
Shellback: Pearl crystal flash over which is a piece of opaque plastic soda straw trimmed and secured at the hook eye
Rib: Copper wire
Tail: Butt of the crystal flash and soda straw pulled down over the hook eye and trimmed
Note: Coat the straw with epoxy cement and pick out the dubbing fur on the bottom to imitate legs.

Tied by Umpqua Feather Merchants

OPOSSUM SHRIMP

Hook: Straight eye, standard length
Tail: Opossum guard hairs with the underfur removed. Once the tail is secured, trim it to a length equal to the hook gape
Body: Opossum underfur, heavy and cigar shaped
Shellback: Clear plastic
Rib: 20 lb. monofilament
Legs: Body dubbing fur picked out
Head: White
Eyes: Painted yellow with a black pupil
Note: The opossum fur used for this pattern is from the cream colored American (not Australian) animal.

Tied by Don Brown

Don Brown of Kingston, Massachusetts, has observed that shrimp drifting in tidal creeks "maintain a straight stick-like body position." Salters and striped bass frequently feed in tidal creeks on shrimp and crustacea, much like trout feed on drifting nymphs.

Tied by Phil Chapman

PHIL'S DAHLBERG SHRIMP

Hook:	Straight eye, long shank	Body:	Blue deer body hair spun and trimmed flat on the bottom and ribbed with soft grizzly hackle clipped on top
Antennae:	Purple bucktail over which is blue crystal flash		
Eyes:	Melted monofilament, dipped in epoxy, with black pupils	Diving collar and head: Purple deer body hair spun and trimmed as shown (the collar must be saturated with cement)	
Legs:	Two blue dyed grizzly and one purple dyed grizzly on each side splayed out, around which are a few turns of soft purple hackle		

Phil Chapman's unusual shrimp may be fished on top, like a Dahlberg Diver, or subsurface where "the bulk of the body and collar pushes lots of water, attracting many strikes."

Tied by Jack Gartside

PIGGYBACK SHRIMP

Hook:	Straight eye, standard length	Body:	Tan-dyed grizzly marabou fluff from the base of saddle hackles, palmered, trimmed on the top and sides
Back:	Three or more small to large gold bead chain "eyes" secured along the top of the hook		
Tail:	Tan-dyed grizzly marabou fluff		

Jack Gartside developed the Piggyback Shrimp to be tied in whatever colors are suitable for imitating your local shrimp. The use of soft marabou plumage creates a fly that looks alive and stays in constant motion.

Tied by Dick Stewart

PFLUEGER HAIR SHRIMP

Hook:	Straight eye, standard length	Head:	Natural deer body hair, spun and trimmed as shown
Body:	Tan dubbing		
Wing:	Sparse white bucktail over which is a little natural deer body hair from the head	Eye:	Silver bead chain or melted monofilament

This bonefish fly has been around for a few years and was designed by Al Pflueger, Jr., who, like his father, was a well known Miami taxidermist and an innovator of saltwater angling techniques.

Tied by Carl Richards

RICHARDS' WHITE SWIMMING SHRIMP

Hook:	Straight eye, long shank		quill and treated with a flexible vinyl cement so the biots stay together
Eyes:	Epoxy balls on monofilament painted amber with black pupils		
Body:	Glassy white yarn or dubbing	Antennae:	White bristle, tinted red on the ends
Legs:	Soft webby fibers from the base of a white hackle, palmered		
Tail:	Polar bear Ultra Hair	Mouth:	Polar bear Ultra Hair extending to about the end of the rostrum
Back:	Polar bear Ultra Hair, with reddish brown markings, ribbed with white thread	Forelegs:	Polar bear Ultra Hair, white body dubbing or yarn, teased out, and a single strand of pearl crystal flash on each side
Rostrum:	A section of biots stripped from the leading edge of a natural goose		

RICHARDS' SNAPPING SHRIMP

Hook: Straight eye, long shank
Mouth and forelegs: Tan Ultra Hair
Eyes: Melted monofilament, painted black pupils
Antennae: 2 long white moose mane hairs or similar
Claws: Liquid latex colored with a marking pen (see Richards' Immature Blue Crab on page 12)

Head and body: Green thread binding down the Ultra Hair from the mouth and forelegs
Legs: Soft webby fibers from the base of a tan hackle, palmered
Back: Tan Ultra Hair
Tail: Tan Ultra Hair tied under the hook eye, leaving a few hairs extending over the hook point

This realistic pattern represents one of the most common shrimps found on bonefish flats.

Tied by Carl Richards

ROOT BEER SHRIMP

Hook: Straight eye, standard length
Body: Root Beer (orange-brown) angora goat, or seal fur substitute applied with a dubbing loop and picked out to look "buggy"
Wing: Root Beer-dyed badger guard hair with the underfur pulled out, or red squirrel tail over which is sparse

copper crystal flash or Flashabou and two Root Beer colored grizzly hackle tips tied on the side
Head: Brown
Note: Jimmy Nix says that to get the color "Root Beer" he dyes his material hot orange with a little blue.

This is an excellent bonefish fly that was designed by Jimmy Nix and detailed in a series of video tapes produced by Jack Dennis. Tied in larger sizes, this fly is also good for redfish.

Tied by Farrow Allen

SASSY SHRIMP

Hook: Straight eye, long shank
Mouth and forelegs: White rabbit fur
Eyes: Silver bead chain with painted black pupils
Underbody: White yarn, tapered
Body: Pearl Mylar tubing, secured front and back with neutral thread,

unravelled over the eye of the hook to form a tail, and at the bend as part of the mouth and forelegs
Rib: Transparent sewing thread
Note: The completed fly may be bent as shown and coated with epoxy.

The Sassy Shrimp is a bonefish fly designed by Joe Butorac, who ties it in "basic white" as shown, and uses waterproof marking pens when color is desired.

Tied by Joe Butorac

SCATES' SHRIMP

Hook: Straight eye, standard length
Weedguard: Stiff monofilament
Antennae and mouth: Yellow bucktail around which is sparse natural deer body hair
Eyes: Melted monofilament painted black or red
Head and abdomen: Yellow chenille

Legs: Black hackle, trimmed from the upper half of the body
Shellback: Yellow crystal flash
Tail: Butts of the yellow crystal flash used to make the shellback pulled down and clipped short as shown
Note: Also tied in red and fluorescent white.

Developed for redfish and seatrout on the Texas flats by Chuck Scates, who operates Shallow Water Guide Service out of South Padre Island.

Tied by Chuck Scates

Tied by Ken Hanley

Tied by Florida Keys Outfitters

Tied by Ken Hanley

Tied by Jim Stewart

SCREAMIN' SHRIMP

Hook: Straight eye, standard length
Antennae: White bucktail over which is orange crystal flash, secured with fluorescent red thread. Don't trim the crystal flash or bucktail as they form the carapace and tail
Eyes: Silver bead chain, on the bottom
Underbody: Red tying thread, tapered as shown, binding down the white bucktail for the lower part of the tail
Body: Clear V-Rib or Larva Lace
Shellback: Orange crystal flash
Tail: Orange crystal flash over white bucktail, trimmed as shown
Rib: Gold or copper wire

"This is one of the hottest patterns I've seen for surfperch," says Ken Hanley, who won't take credit for developing this fly, but spent a few years and countless fishing hours experimenting to confirm that red was the most productive color.

SNAPPING SHRIMP, BROWN

Hook: Straight eye, standard length
Butt: Orange yarn or chenille
Body: Tan dubbing or chenille
Wing: Brown craft fur over pearl crystal flash
Head: Black

This is a simple to tie and effective bonefish fly for areas of turtle grass where small snapping shrimp frequently hide. All snapping shrimp are easily identified by their oversized fighting claw and smaller feeding claw. When disturbed, it's larger claw will snap together resulting in a snapping noise that can be heard both in and out of the water. This version was designed by Chico Fernandez of Miami.

SLACKWATER SHRIMP

Hook: Straight eye, standard length
Antennae: White bucktail, secured with white tying thread as shown
Eyes: Silver bead chain, on top of the hook
Body: Pearl-Blue Flash Lite Brite, dubbed
Beard: Gold Flashabou, as long as the white bucktail
Collar: Yellow hackle
Head: White

Ken Hanley of Fremont, California, designed this fly that's most productive at dead high slack tide around rocky shoreline structure, bridges or piers. From southern Oregon to northern Baja, it's accounted for most species of surfperch and rockfish. Hanley is the author of *California Fly Tying & Fishing Guide*, and teaches a popular outdoor course in surf fly fishing.

STEWART'S SHRIMP-A-ROO

Hook: Straight eye, long shank
Antennae: Four strands of black crystal flash
Mouth and forelegs: A short fluorescent orange hackle and three dark furnace hackles on each side, curving out, with gold crystal flash over the top and a ball of fluorescent orange chenille
Body: Fluorescent orange and natural gray deer body hair stacked over white deer body hair and trimmed as shown, cemented on the bottom and the diving face
Eyes: One half of a solid black plastic bead cemented on each side

This impressionistic shrimp of Jim Stewart's floats and dives and has accounted for a lot of shallow-water redfish, seatrout and snook.

TARPON SHRIMP

Hook: Straight eye, standard length
Wing: Six grizzly hackles curving out
Eyes: 50 lb. monofilament dipped in brown colored epoxy
Collar: Natural badger hair or bleached gray squirrel, tied sparse. Then short badger underfur
Head: Pearl Frost Brite or Mylar coated with epoxy
Note: Before tying the wing of this or any other traditional tarpon fly, Nix adds a "snarzle" to help prevent the wing from fouling. A "snarzle" is the name Flip Pallot gave to a stiff hackle stem tied in the tail position.

This is a large shrimp pattern that Jimmy Nix likes to use for big tarpon.

Tied by Umpqua Feather Merchants

TERMIN-ATOR SHRIMP

Hook: Straight eye, standard length
Antennae: Light moose mane and pearlescent orange crystal flash
Mouth and forelegs: Black Twinkle or crystal hair, mixed dark and light moose mane and one long and short grizzly hackle on each side curving out
Rostrum: Natural brown bucktail
Eyes: Melted mono dipped in epoxy
Head: Long fiber orange crystal chenille
Legs: Several grizzly hackles, palmered over the thorax and trimmed
Abdomen: Mottled brown and dark brown deer body hair, spun and trimmed as shown, leaving some long hairs on the bottom
Tail: Deer hair or moose mane tied under the hook, colored brown, lacquered and trimmed to look like tail spines

First tied for tarpon in 1987 by Phil Chapman, this fly measures over four inches long.

Tied by Phil Chapman

ULTRA SHRIMP

Hook: Straight eye, standard length
Underbody: Tan thread
Forelegs: Tan Ultra Hair, pointing down
Body: Tan Ultra Hair, cocking up slightly, tapered to a point, over which is optional gold crystal flash. Leave two long Ultra Hair fibers untrimmed to imitate antennae
Eyes: Melted monofilament
Legs: Light ginger or badger hackle palmered over the head and trimmed on top
Tail: Tan Ultra Hair
Back: Ultra Hair from the tail pulled forward, trimmed to a point over the head and epoxied

Bob Popovic's Ultra Shrimp is fairly easy to tie and very durable. You can modify the color and size to match any shrimp that swims.

Tied by Bob Popovics

VISIBLE SHRIMP

Hook: Straight eye, standard length
Antennae: A mixture of half a dozen light and dark Chinese boar bristles or moose mane fibers
Shellback and tail: White poly-yarn
Head: Yellow floss
Abdomen: Yellow seal fur or substitute, picked out on bottom
Rib: Yellow Pseudo-Quill
Eyes: Hollow plastic

Designed for bonefish by Ed Davis of Ontario, Canada. Davis is convinced that being able to see your fly in the water is as important as being able to see the fish to which you are casting. The contrast of this yellow fly against dark bottoms adds to its visibility. For white sand bottoms one should tie this fly with dark materials.

Tied by Ed Davis

Other Bonefish

Tied by Winston Moore

Tied by Tony Route

Tied by Farrow Allen

AGENT ORANGE

Hook: Straight eye, standard length
Underbody: Lead wire (optional)
Body: Orange sparkle chenille (chenille with a tinsel core)
Wing: Hot orange FisHair outside of which are two grizzly hackle tips on each side

Winston Moore's Agent Orange has always been deadly in the Bahamas; moreover "the larger fish (over 10 lbs.) seem to especially prefer it." At Charlie's Haven, before the Crazy Charlie became popular, the Agent Orange was considered their most productive bonefish fly.

ALMOST NOTHING

Hook: Straight eye, standard length
Body: Pearlescent Mylar tinsel
Wing: Pearl crystal flash

Tony Route of Anchorage, Alaska, developed this fly in Florida in 1979 for spooky bonefish. The very first flies were dressed ". . . with the unidentified remnants . . . found in an Easter basket." They worked, but fell apart quickly. Tied with crystal flash, the Almost Nothing has been a durable pattern that takes shy bonefish in Florida, the Caribbean and South Pacific.

BAITED BREATH

Hook: Straight eye, standard length
Antennae and forelegs: On the bend several long dark brown marabou barbs surrounded by tan marabou
Eyes: Bead chain painted black and secured on top opposite the barb
Legs: Ginger variant hackle wrapped between the antennae and eyes
Body: Yellow and brown(or black) variegated chenille, built up at the eyes and tapering towards the hook eye

This fly was developed by Robert McCurdy of Austin, Texas. It sits on the bottom with the hook point up; the marabou waves about.

Tied by Tim Borski

Tied by Dick Stewart

Tied by Florida Keys Outfitters

BONEFISH SLIDER

Hook: Straight eye, standard length
Wing: Clear craft fur hair barred with an olive waterproof marking pen, over which is pearlescent crystal flash
Hackle: Long soft grizzly, palmered over the rear half of the hook and trimmed on the bottom
Eyes: Lead, yellow with black pupils
Collar: Dark deer body hair, on top only
Head: Natural dark and light deer body hair, spun and trimmed flat. The finished head should look mottled and coloration can be added with a marking pen

Tim Borski says of his Slider "that bonefish have picked it off the bottom as it sat still."

BONEFISH SPECIAL

Hook: Straight eye, standard length
Tail: Orange marabou, short
Underbody: Flat gold Mylar tinsel
Body: Clear monofilament
Wing: White bucktail or calftail over which are two grizzly hackles

A popular bonefish fly that was designed by Chico Fernandez of Miami. Lefty Kreh considers it an important fly that "every bonefisherman should carry."

CLOUSER KEYS MINNOW

Hook: Straight eye, standard length
Eyes: Lead eyes painted white with black pupils and secured with fluorescent green thread
Throat: White bucktail
Wing: Chartreuse crystal flash over which is fluorescent green bucktail, all very sparse

This small, sparse variation of Bob Clouser's Deep Minnow streamer (which see) has become a popular bonefish fly in the Florida Keys.

Tied by Mike Wolverton

FLATS MASTER

Hook: Straight eye, standard shank
Tail: Orange marabou
Body: Fluorescent orange nylon
Wing: Tan or medium brown craft fur
Collar: Two turns of soft grizzly hackle
Eyes: Silver bead chain (optional)
Head: Fluorescent orange nylon, built up

Mike Wolverton designed this pattern for bonefish and first fished it in 1980. Wolverton describes it as a durable, easy to tie fly that "catches lots of fish." This dressing is the original, but in recent years the Flats Master has proven itself in yellow, white, chartreuse and pink.

Tied by Dick Stewart

FRANKEE-BELLE

Hook: Straight eye, standard length
Body: Fluorescent green chenille, heavy
Wing: Fine white bucktail, taken from the tip of the tail, outside of which are two narrow grizzly hackles
Head: Red

Developed in the 1940s by Frankee Albright, one of the only women licensed as a Florida guide, and Belle Mathers of Miami. This fly qualifies as one of the oldest bonefish flies still in use. The fly is usually tied with a reverse-wing and the hook point up, although it was not originated this way. Early examples had a white body and brown wing.

Tied by George Hommell

HOMMELL'S BONEFISH

Hook: Straight eye, standard length
Body: Heavy cerise floss, overwrapped with monofilament and cemented
Wing: Fine white rabbit fur
Head: Heavy cerise floss
Eyes: Small hollow plastic eyes, cemented to the head

Tied in many colors, this fly (which has also been called the Evil Eye) was developed in the early 1980s by George Hommell of the World Wide Sportsman, in Islamorada, Florida. Hommell, who began his guiding career in 1952, has guided many anglers, including President George Bush.

Tied by Dick Stewart

HORROR

Hook: Straight eye, standard length
Body: None. Some variations call for a yellow chenille body.
Wing: Natural brown bucktail
Head: Yellow chenille secured with black thread

The Horror was developed many years ago by Pete Perinchief and is generally believed to be one of the earliest successful "reverse-wing" flies used for bonefish. It is said that Perinchief named it the Horror after his headstrong young daughter. Now, of course, nearly all bonefish flies are tied so the hook point is up.

Tied by Dick Stewart

LEE CUDDY BONEFISH

Hook: Straight eye, standard length
Body: White chenille
Wing: Red bucktail over which is white bucktail flanked by a grizzly hackle on each side
Head: Fluorescent red

An older bonefish fly that is still quite effective and popular.

Tied by Lenny Moffo

LENNY'S CRUSTACEAN

Hook: Straight eye, standard length
Tail: Brown marabou outside of which are 2 cree hackles curving out
Underbody: Lead wire fastened to the top of the hook shank
Legs: White rubber hackle, painted as shown
Eyes: Glass
Body: Gray synthetic and natural dubbing, tapering towards the head

Lenny Moffo refers to this generic bonefish fly as a "buggy looking guy that looks like food." Moffo always paints the rubber hackle when using it for legs; he believes that the fish see them better.

Other Bonefish

Tied by Dan Johnson

Tied by Redding Fly Shop

Tied by Jon Olch

McVAY'S GOTCHA

Hook: Straight eye, standard length
Tail: Pearl Flashabou
Eyes: Silver bead chain or chromed lead
Body: Pearl Diamond Braid, up to and barely in front of the eyes
Wing: Sparse pearl crystal flash over which is pale tan craft fur
Head: Pink

Developed by Jim McVay, who has taken many large Andros Island bonefish on this design.

MINI PUFF, PINK

Hook: Straight eye, standard length
Eyes: Small silver bead chain
Wing: Brown calftail over which are a pair of grizzly hackle tips curving out
Head: Fluorescent pink chenille

This is a popular color combination for this important bonefish fly, although it's good in a variety of other colors. The fly's weight can be increased by using lead dumbbell eyes.

PEARL MOTIVATOR

Hook: Straight eye, standard length
Underbody: Lead wire
Tail: Tan rabbit fur and two ginger variant hackle tips
Eyes: Oversized silver bead chain
Body: Fine pearlescent braided Mylar tinsel, wrapped around and in front of the bead chain eyes
Note: After the head has been finished, Olch dips or coats the body and eyes with clear Insta-Dip, a rubbery substance used for coating tool handles.

Tied by Dick Stewart

Tied by Jack Gartside

Tied by The Fly Fisherman

PUFF

Hook: Straight eye, standard length
Tail: Four cree or ginger variant hackles curving out, veiled by natural badger or opossum guard hairs
Skirt: Soft black hackle
Eyes: Glass, or painted lead eyes if more weight is needed
Head: Tan chenille

Developed by veteran Florida Keys guide Nat Ragland, and well known as the first fly that permit would eat with any consistency. It's still a good permit fly though its popularity has been eclipsed by a host of successful crab imitations. In small sizes the Puff is an excellent bonefish fly. Puffs, or the similar Woodstock pattern, are tied in many colors.

SPARROW

Hook: Straight eye, standard length
Tail: Grizzly marabou (rump) dyed tan
Body: Tan rabbit, poly, antron or a blended dubbing
Hackle: Ringneck pheasant rump, wrapped like a collar
Eyes: Gold or silver bead chain
Head: Ringneck pheasant aftershafts wrapped behind, between and in front of the eyes

The Sparrow was originated by Jack Gartside for freshwater fishing. As a bonefish pattern Gartside says it ". . . doesn't specifically imitate any one food, but is suggestive of many. If I had one bonefish fly to fish, this would be it." Tan and orange seem to be the best colors.

TWO FEATHER FLY

Hook: Straight eye, standard length
Eyes: Silver bead chain
Tail: Brown-orange grizzly hackle tips curving out
Body: Brown-orange grizzly fluff from the base of the same hackle palmered over the body
Wing: Sparse brown bucktail

Liz Steele of The Fly Fisherman in Titusville, Florida, got this pattern from Bob LeMay of Miami. It's been an excellent producer for bonefish and is frequently tied in gray or other subdued colors.

Tied by Bob Nauheim

CRAZY CHARLIE

Eyes: Silver bead chain
Tail: Silver Flashabou
Underbody: Silver Flashabou
Overbody: 15 lb. to 20 lb. clear monofilament
Wing: Two white or off-white hackle tips

Tied by Bob Nauheim

HAIRWING CHARLIE

Eyes: Silver bead chain
Tail: Silver Flashabou
Underbody: Silver Flashabou
Overbody: 15 lb. to 20 lb. clear monofilament
Wing: Fine white hair

Tied by Joe Branham

EPOXY CHARLIE

Eyes: Silver bead chain or lead eyes
Body: Pearl crystal flash, epoxy over
Wing: White calftail over which is pearl crystal flash plus two grizzly hackle tips on each side curving in

Tied by Florida Keys Outfitters

BROWN & GOLD CHARLIE

Eyes: Gold bead chain
Body: Flat gold tinsel over which is a coat of epoxy cement or monofilament
Wing: Brown calftail

Tied by Florida Keys Outfitters

PINK CHARLIE

Eyes: Silver bead chain
Body: Pearl Flashabou over which is a coat of epoxy cement or monofilament
Wing: Pink calftail
Head: Pink

Tied by Joe Branham

PINK FLASH

Weight: Lead tape or foil on top of the hook
Underbody: Pink floss or thread
Eyes: Silver bead chain
Overbody: Clear Swannundaze
Wing: Pearl Flashabou

Tied by Bob Nauheim

FORGETFUL CHARLIE

Head: Silver bead chain secured with fluorescent green thread
Body: Fluorescent green Amnesia monofilament
Wing: Pearlescent green crystal flash

Tied by Fishing International

MAX'S CHARLIE

Eyes: Silver bead chain, secured with white thread
Body: Pearlescent green crystal flash
Wing: Pearlescent green crystal flash

Tied by Fishing International

YUCATAN CHARLIE

Eyes: Silver bead chain, secured with fluorescent green thread
Tail: Pink Glo-bug yarn
Body: Fluorescent green Amnesia monofilament
Wing: Fine white hair

Tied by David Caprera

4C'S FLATS FLY

Hook:	Straight eye, standard length		thread
Body:	Epoxy or Plastidip, an opaque rubbery cement that is sold in hardware stores for coating tool handles. Body is coated over a frame built with 15 lb. monofilament that is secured in front, looped back on each side and tied off with red	Eyes:	Bead chain or lead buckshot set into the body as it hardens
		Wing:	Cream FisHair outside of which are two grizzly hackle tips curving in and pearl crystal flash over
		Head:	Cream

The 4C's is Dave Caprera's answer to the all purpose fly that works well on the flats. His unique construction method simplifies the forming of the epoxy or cement-filled body.

Tied by Tim Borski

BONEFISH SHORT, TAN

Hook:	Straight eye, standard length		monofilament positioned at the mid-point of the hook shank
Tail:	Light tan calftail over which is orange crystal flash	Head:	Wrap gold Mylar tinsel on front half of hook shank. Form a flat, triangular shaped head with epoxy, from the eyes forward
Skirt:	Grizzly hackle, long and webby		
Wing:	Two short grizzly hackle tips tied flat and delta wing style		
Eyes:	Glass beads, strung on stiff		

Tim Borski is a wildlife artist who lives in Islamorada, Florida, and fishes "an average of 6 days a week—four on a bad week." He created this epoxy fly in the late 1980s. Borski says that "day in and day out, this is the most effective epoxy fly I've ever thrown at bonefish." He ties a white variation that he fishes over sandy bottoms, while the tan one is used in grass.

Tied by Joe Branham

EPOXY MINI-PUFF

Hook:	Straight eye, standard length	Eyes:	Silver bead chain, or chromed lead dumbbell eyes
Wing:	White calftail over which are several strands of pearl crystal flash plus two grizzly hackle tips on each side curving in	Head:	Wraps of pearl crystal flash, around the eyes, built up with epoxy

This variation of the standard chenille-head Mini-Puff was first tied by Joe Branham of Valdosta, Georgia, in the late 1980s. Branham is a commercial fly tier whose flies are as durable as they are effective.

Tied by Jack Montague

EPOXY PERMIT FLY

Hook:	Straight eye, standard length		When dry paint the bottom cream.
Tail:	Tan FishFuzz, outside of which are two cock ringneck pheasant body feathers curving outward	Eyes:	Red metallic sequins with painted black pupils cemented over the bead chain. The entire head, including the eyes, is coated with epoxy
Head:	Tie in a pair of large silver bead chain eyes and build up the head with two coats of tinted epoxy.		

Designed in the early 1980s by Jack Montague of Punta Gorda, Florida. Montague also ties a nearly identical smaller fly for bonefish.

ERIC'S EPOXY BONEFISH FLY, YELLOW

Wing: Gold craft fur outside of which are 2 gold-grizzly hackles curving in
Skirt: Gold deer body hair
Eyes: Gold bead chain with black pupils
Head: Make a frame for the head of fine 2 lb. monofilament and fill with Mod Podge, a waterproof craft glue that dries clear. Once the Mod Podge is dry, apply tinted epoxy to the bottom of the fly, let it cure, then turn the fly over. Heat one end of a mono weedguard, set in place and secure with an epoxy coat to the top side

Eric Peterson's technique of applying epoxy over a Mod Podge base makes it unnecessary to rotate the fly while the epoxy cures.

Tied by Eric Pererson

LENNY'S BUCKSHOT BONEFISH FLY

Tail: Pearl crystal flash over which is white marabou outside of which are grizzly hackle tips curving out
Head: Built up with pink epoxy to a kite shape, wrapped with pearl Flashabou or crystal flash, and again coated with pink epoxy
Eyes: Lead shot, set into the epoxy before it cures; a final epoxy coat over the eyes and head
Note: To choose the proper size lead shot, use approximately the same size shot as hook. For example: on a size 6 fly use size 6 shot.

Moffo often uses lead shot for the eyes of his bonefish flies and simply increases the size of the shot if he feels the need for more weight. As a guide he ties a lot of flies and lead shot is inexpensive.

Tied by Lenny Moffo

NIX'S BROWN EPOXY BONEFISH

Tail: Red squirrel tail outside of which are sparse strands of copper crystal flash
Weedguard: Double strands of stiff monofilament set just behind the eye of the hook
Head: Diamond shaped epoxy tinted brown with painted black eyes

This is a fairly simple weedless epoxy fly thats easy to tie. For beginners in epoxy fly tying the diamond shape can be achieved by any one of several methods: making a mold, building a monofilament frame, or forming a shape from clear sheet plastic.

Tied by Umpqua Feather Merchants

TAILER MAID

Hook: Straight eye, standard length
Tail: Pearl crystal flash over which is natural brown hair with a tan speckled rubber hackle on each side
Body: Several brown hackles palmered over a thread base saturated with CA glue. After the hackle has been wrapped, spray with "Kicker", and trim as shown when dry
Body and weedguard: A piece of clear Mylar is cut to form the diamond shape of the head and the weedguard. Secure the head portion to the underside of the hook and crimp mini lead split shot in place for the eyes, tint brown, and coat with epoxy. Pull the Mylar weedguard back, punch a hole at the back, and pull over the hook point
Note: If the Mylar weedguard proves troublesome, substitute a traditional one, or eliminate it.

Tied by A. J. Hand

A.J. Hand's Tailer Maid has accounted for many big bonefish and may be tied in a variety of colors. Orange ones with a lot of gold flash in the tail are deadly on redfish.

Barracuda Flies

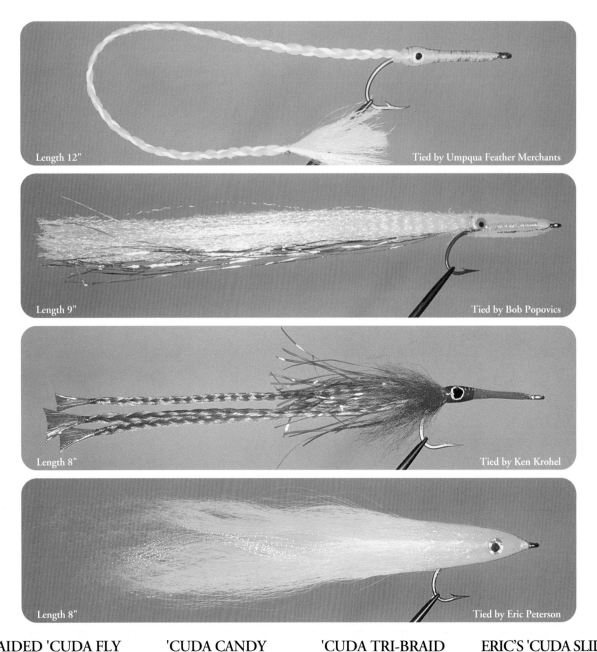

Length 12"   Tied by Umpqua Feather Merchants

Length 9"   Tied by Bob Popovics

Length 8"   Tied by Ken Krohel

Length 8"   Tied by Eric Peterson

BRAIDED 'CUDA FLY

Body: Braided FisHair: two parts fluorescent green and one part white

Tail: Fluorescent green and white FisHair, tied off and spread out as shown

Head: Fluorescent green

Eyes: Painted white with a black pupil, solid or hollow plastic eyes

This is a long needlefish imitation that may be tied as long or as short as needed.

'CUDA CANDY

Wing: Silver Flashabou, fluorescent green Ultra Hair over

Body: Silver Flashabou wrapped over the hook shank; the balance of the crystal hair pulled forward and secured in front, all saturated with epoxy mixed with sparkle flakes

Eyes: Peel-off, stick-on orange with black pupils

Lateral line: Green marking pen

Note: Add a final light coat of epoxy over the body.

'CUDA TRI-BRAID

Body: Three sets of braided orange nylon

Tails: Tie off each set of braided nylon, flatten, cement with epoxy and paint fluorescent orange

Collar: Orange pearlescent Flashabou over which is orange calftail

Head: Red, a painted yellow eye with a black pupil and a fluorescent orange tip

Ken Krohel says his Tri-Braid pattern has a lot of action that often appeals to sullen barracuda.

ERIC'S 'CUDA SLIDER

Tail: Chartreuse crystal flash over which is a collar of hot yellow bucktail

Body: A hot yellow bucktail collar at both the middle and front of the shank

Wing: Hot green streamer hair tied in front and laying over the 3 bucktail collars

Head: Silicone rubber over the streamer hair to a point beyond the bend. Keep the head hollow

Eyes: Peel-off prismatic eyes

Note: Full name is Eric's Green 'Cuda Tube Slider.

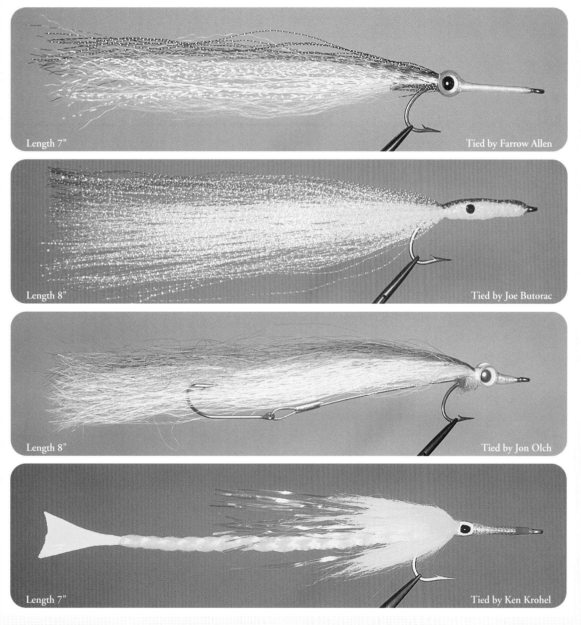

Length 7" — Tied by Farrow Allen

Length 8" — Tied by Joe Butorac

Length 8" — Tied by Jon Olch

Length 7" — Tied by Ken Krohel

KEY WEST 'CUDA KILLER		KRYSTAL 'KUDA		NEEDLEFISH, GREEN		WHO'S HOO	
Wing:	Fine soft fluorescent green hair, over which are about a dozen strands of white, half as much fluorescent green, and about eight strands each of pink and blue crinkled synthetic hair, with sparse peacock crystal flash over all	Underbody:	White yarn	Front hook:	Size 2/0 straight eye	Body:	Braided chartreuse nylon
		Wing:	Tied Thunder Creek style: a large bunch of chartreuse Krystal Flash surrounding and covering the yarn underbody, topped with peacock Krystal Flash and secured at the bend with transparent sewing thread	Trailing hook:	Size 1/0 straight eye, connected by a strand of 40 lb. stainless wire, hook point up	Tail:	Tie off the nylon braid, flatten, epoxy, trim into the shape of a fish tail and paint fluorescent green
				Butt:	Red yarn and fluorescent green synthetic dubbing	Collar:	Pearlescent Flashabou over which is fluorescent green Fish Fuzz or similar
Cheeks:	Red crystal flash			Wing:	White over which is light green over which is dark green synthetic hair	Head:	Fluorescent green Mylar tubing, painted white eye with a black pupil, and a hot orange tip. Epoxy
Head:	Fluorescent green	Eyes:	Painted yellow with a black pupil	Head:	Fluorescent green floss, built up		
Eyes:	Solid plastic	Note:	As a final step, coat head with epoxy cement.	Eyes:	Hollow plastic	Note:	Krohel ties 'cuda flies up to a foot long..
Note:	Coat the entire head and the eyes with epoxy.			Note:	Dip the head in Plasti-Dip.		
Jimmy Nix likes to throw the Key West 'Cuda Killer at big barracuda.		Developed for barracuda by Joe Butorac, this fly is very durable.					

Length 5"   Tied by Joe Blados

Length 3"   Tied by Tim Borski

Length 4"   Tied by Jim Buckingham

CREASE FLY SQUID

Hook: Straight eye, long shank
Tentacles and antennae: Pale pink marabou
    barbs outside of which are long nar-
    row white badger saddle hackles over
    which are strands of pink crystal flash
Eyes: Peel-off, stick-on prismatic eyes
Body: Live Body foam trimmed to shape
    and secured to the hook with Zap-A-
    Gap CA glue (see Crease Fly Min-
    now) and painted as shown with
    waterproof marking pens and coated
    with epoxy

Joe Blados of Southhold, New York, has con-
trived a realistic looking group of minnows,
crabs and squid using Livebody Foam, Zap-A-
Gap, marking pens and epoxy.

EPOXY OCTOPUS

Hook: Straight eye, standard length
Tentacles: Pale gray-tan calftail over which is
    pearl crystal flash and a mix of 6 grizzly,
    cree, and ginger variant hackles
Mouth: Gold-olive crystal chenille
Eyes: Glass taxidermy
Head: Build up the hook shank with wraps
    of gold Mylar tinsel, around and in
    front of the glass eyes. Construct a
    symmetrical frame of heavy
    monofilament running from the
    hook eye to each glass eye, and fill
    with epoxy tinted light amber

Tim Borski began designing this fly after catching
"... a large mutton snapper that had eleven small
brown octopi in its stomach." He also uses pink or
white for offshore dorado, kingfish and blackfin
tuna. It's difficult to construct, but worthwhile.

JIM BUCK SQUID

Hook: Straight eye, long shank
Tentacles: Pink marabou, pearlescent crystal
    flash on the top and bottom sur-
    rounded by a "collar" of eight cerise
    hackles, all curving outward
Eyes: Clear glass eyes, set on the top of
    the hook shank to help make the fly
    turn over and ride hook point up
Body: Hot pink chenille, wrapped around the
    eyes, tapering towards the hook eye
Rib: Long fiber crystal chenille (optional)
Note: For dorado, Buckingham likes char-
    treuse tentacles with a dark green
    body; while the pink versions are
    good for small tuna.

First tied in 1966 by Jim Buckingham. Before crystal flash became available,
Buckingham used braided Mylar.

Length 5" Tied by Dan Blanton

Length 4" Tied by Bob Popovics

Length 3" Tied by John Shewey

SEA ARROW SQUID

Hook: Straight eye, long shank
Beak: Gold braid tinsel followed by a turn of white chenille
Tentacles: Sparse purple bucktail, 10 speckled white hackles curving out (the outermost hackles are much longer) outside of which is sparse purple crystal flash (hackles are spotted black and rust)
Eyes: Solid glass or plastic
Head: White marabou applied like a collar
Body: Cream chenille, spotted
Tail fins: On each side a bunch of white calftail over which is pearl crystal flash

Dan Blanton tied the first Sea Arrow Squid in 1969. The name derives from the arrow shaped tail fin he formed by saturating yarn with silicone rubber sealant and trimming it to shape. This is Blanton's current variation.

SILI-SQUID, LIME

Hook: Straight eye, long shank
Tentacles: Fluorescent green speckled rubber hackle
Eyes: Solid glass taxidermy eyes on a stem
Underbody: Long fiber pearlescent crystal chenille and enough lamb's wool to hold the silicone and form the tail fins
Overbody: Clear silicone rubber tinted lime green and spread over the the underbody, shaped and sprinkled with glitter flakes (to form the arrow shaped tail fins work the silicone into the lamb's wool, shape and trim)
Note: Add a final silicone coat to head and fins.

This fly is tied mainly for inshore fishing. Popovics also ties a larger offshore version that uses long saddle hackles for tentacles, speckled with a marking pen.

SQUIRMING SQUID

Hook: Straight eye, standard length
Tail: Pearl Flashabou
Butt: Long fiber white crystal chenille
Tentacles: A collar of pearl Flashabou and white rubber hackle
Body: Long fiber white crystal chenille
Head: Chrome lead dumbbell eyes secured with fluorescent red thread

When schools of small squid invade bays from northern California to southern British Columbia, the impressionistic Shewey's Squirming Squid is deadly for most species of rockfish. Shewey says that it "should be retrieved with two or three quick strips followed by a pause." Rockfish often eat this squid during the pause as it sinks.

Worms

Length 5"   Tied by Jack Gartside

BRISTLEWORM

Hook: Straight eye, long or standard length
Body: Two matched narrow dark furnace saddle hackles, tied flat, curving away from one another including some base fluff
Head: Rusty orange dubbing, picked out to look like legs (bristles)

Bristleworms (clamworms, sandworms, seaworms) are a favorite choice of inshore live bait fishermen along the east coast. The worms are mostly nocturnal feeders and are commonly found around mudflats and mussel beds, where stripers often come to search for them after dark. This is a convincing imitation from Jack Gartside.

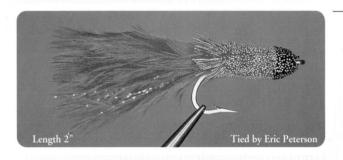

Length 2"   Tied by Eric Peterson

CINDER WORM

Hook: Straight eye, standard length
Tail: Sparse orange crystal flash over which is red marabou
Body: Red deer body hair spun and trimmed
Head: Black deer body hair spun and trimmed

During exceptionally high late night tides that occur during the new and full phases of the moon, hatches of sandworms swarm out of tidal marshes and estuaries along the northern Atlantic coast and striped bass move inshore to gorge on them. Eric Peterson's Cinder Worm creates a surface disturbance that gets the attention of bass feeding in the midst of thousands of naturals.

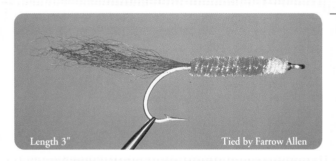

Length 3"   Tied by Farrow Allen

PALOLO WORM

Hook: Straight eye, long shank
Tail: Bright orange calftail, one inch long
Body: Fluorescent orange chenille
Head: Tan chenille

At various time in the tropical waters, tremendous "hatches" of these small worms occur, driving tarpon crazy and sending them into feeding frenzies. Lefty Kreh thinks that this is the best imitation.

Length 2 1/2"   Tied by Lenny Moffo

PALOLO WORM

Hook: Straight eye, standard length
Body: Fluorescent orange thread surrounded by bright orange bucktail
Collar: Fluorescent green hackle
Head: Fluorescent green coated with epoxy
Eyes: Black

This is Lenny Moffo's pattern for imitating the palolo worm found in the Florida Keys. This is a pretty convincing fly in the water, that has taken its share of tarpon during "the hatch."

Length 3"   Tied by Lou Tabory

TABORY'S WORM HATCH FLY

Hook: Straight eye, standard length
Wing: White marabou over which is pink-orange marabou
Head and collar: Pink-orange deer body hair spun and trimmed fairly full

Lou Tabory describes this as a variation of his Snake Fly (which see). It's tied on a smaller hook with a proportionally larger head to imitate a sandworm swimming at the surface of the water.

BOB'S BANGER

Hook: Straight eye, long shank
Tail: White bucktail
Skirt: Long fiber pearl crystal chenille
Popper body: Dense red Livebody foam covered with glitter tape, drilled
        through the center and slipped over the hook, but not cemented
Eyes: Peel-off, stick-on prismatic eyes
Note: Although you may cement the popping head in place, Popovics
        suggests leaving it unsecured so you can easily interchange differ-
        ent color heads.

This fly is easy to tie and cast. The resiliency of the "Livebody" helps Bob's
Bangers resist attack from toothy gamefish, and continue floating high.

Tied by Bob Popovics

BOILERMAKER

Hook: Straight eye, long shank
Tail: White bucktail over which is pearl crystal flash over which is red
        bucktail
Popper body: Tapered closed cell foam with a deeply cupped face
Eyes: Solid plastic
Note: Edgewater also manufactures this popper body with a built in
        rattle chamber.

Preformed, prepainted, ready-to-use bodies or complete popper kits are sold
through fly-tying shops.

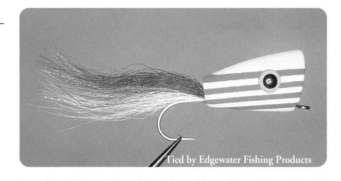
Tied by Edgewater Fishing Products

DINK

Hook: Straight eye, long shank
Tail: Yellow marabou over which is pearl crystal flash
Popper body: Yellow closed cell foam with a deeply cupped face
Eyes: Solid plastic

This small popper was developed for redfish and has also been effective for
small striped bass and blufish feeding in saltwater tidal ponds and creeks.

Tied by Edgewater Fishing Products

GURGLER

Hook: Straight eye, standard length
Tail: Sparse white bucktail mixed with rainbow crinkle Mylar
Body: Closed cell foam
Rib: White thread, securing the foam, forming 5 equal segments
Hackle: Grizzly, palmered
Shellback: Closed cell foam, over which are the butt ends of the tail material
Head: Closed cell foam, trimmed as shown
Note: To make a slider simply trim the foam head tight to the hook.
        Foam may also be colored with a marking pen
"By far this is my favorite surface fly for stripers and blues," says Jack Gartside
of Boston, Massachusetts. "It falls somewhere between the popper and the
slider." It's easy to tie and doesn't demand a lot of effort to cast. It works well
on shy fish which might otherwise be spooked by a large, noisy popper.

Tied by Jack Gartside

Casting Poppers

Tied by Brooks Bouldin

MYLAR POPPER

Hook: Straight eye, long or kinked shank
Tail: White bucktail over which is pearlescent green crystal flash and green bucktail
Underbody: Plain white popper body secured to the hook and painted dark green or blue on top
Body: Braided Mylar tubing or Flashabou Minnow Body pulled over the the underbody, unravel some braid to become a part of the tail and saturate with epoxy or CA cement. Trim at face
Eyes: Hollow plastic
Popper face: Painted red and white
Brooks Bouldin of the Angler's Edge in Houston, sent us this popular surface fly that his customers use for redfish and seatrout along the Texas flats.

PENCIL POPPER

Hook: Straight eye, long shank or special kinked popper style hook
Tail: Six to eight white hackles curving out
Skirt: White hackle
Body: Cork or foam, secured to the hook and dipped or painted as shown, or as desired
Eyes: Painted or peel off or solid plastic or hollow plastic

Tied by Edgewater Fishing Products

This is a basic saltwater popper that can be painted as elaborately or as simply as you choose. For cruising redfish in skinny water you'll want a fairly realistic paint job, while for bluefish in the surf it doesn't matter as long as it's moving.

SEA FOAM POPPER, YELLOW

Hook: Straight eye, long kinked shank
Tail: White bucktail over which is yellow crystal flash over which is fluorescent yellow bucktail
Popper body: Molded yellow (Sea Foam) closed cell foam with a slightly cupped face
Eyes: Hollow plastic

Tied by Mystic Bay Flies

Developed by A.J. Hand and Mystic Bay Flies to be light, float high in the water, and "cast better than any other popper of it's size." A fluorescent green version is effective on Cape Cod stripers. This design is similar to the older Ka-Boom-Boom popper.

SPINSTER

Hook: Straight eye, standard length
Tail: Yellow marabou over which is pearl crystal flash and red bucktail with two yellow hackles curving out, and a small bunch of red marabou on each side
Popper body: Yellow closed cell foam. Basically a popper head filed flat on the bottom and turned around so the small end faces forward
Eyes: Solid plastic

Tied by Edgewater Fishing Products

Designed by Edgewater Fishing Products as a surface slider to imitate a dying minnow trying to dive below the surface.

BEACH BUG

Hook:	Straight eye, standard length
Tag:	Gold or copper braided poly flash
Eyes:	Silver bead chain or chromed lead dumbbell eyes mounted on the top of the shank to help the point ride up
Body:	Fluorescent orange chenille fol- lowed by gold or copper braided poly flash built up around the eyes
Wing:	White calftail or synthetic hair over which is orange hair with grizzly hackle tips on each side
Head:	Epoxy over orange thread

Tied by Nick Curcione

This fly was developed by Nick Curcione of Redondo Beach, California, for barred surfperch, halibut and corbina. According to Curcione, a fly fishing pioneer on the west coast, surfperch love to feed on a little crab called a "mole crab" or "sand crab." The Beach Bug imitates the female crab that becomes orange when she's ripe with eggs.

CHUM FLY

Hook:	Straight eye, standard length
Underbody:	Lead wire (optional, different amounts of weight will be needed to drift the fly naturally depending on the speed of the tide)
Tail:	Brown to cream marabou with sparse strands of red marabou on each side
Collar:	Several turns of brown to cream marabou
Note:	Use marabou that approximates the different colors of various dead fish parts that make up your chum stew

Tied by Farrow Allen

There is no doubt that releasing a steady stream of bloody, cut up fish parts (chum) into the tide flow will attract predators within casting range. If this is something you want to try, here's a fly that imitates chum.

EYE FLY

Hook:	Straight eye (bent up slightly), standard length
Tail:	Hot orange marabou outside of which on each side is a single grizzly hackle dyed orange, curving out
Eyes:	Glass taxidermy set on the top side of the hook
Abdomen:	Fluorescent orange thread
Thorax:	Hot orange Braid Flash or similar wrapped over and around the eyes
Note:	Coat entire fly with epoxy. Also tied in pink and fluorescent green

Tied by Farrow Allen

This is a flashy attractor fly that works well on redfish.

KEEL BUGGER, PINK

Hook:	Keel hook or bendback hook, tied hook point up
Tail:	Shell-pink marabou over which is pink Flashabou
Body:	Shell-pink chenille
Rib:	Gold or copper wire
Hackle:	Orange
Head:	Red

Tied by John Shewey

John Shewey tied the Keel Bugger to imitate the common mud shrimp that's abundant on the Pacific Coast. This is an effective, simple-to-tie pattern that has caught everything from rockfish to sea run cutthroat. It is also Shewey's most productive fly for starry flounder.

Tied by Dana Griffin

RED OCTOBER

Hook:	Straight eye, standard length tied hook point up		Cactus) chenille
Tail:	Pearl Flashabou	Wing:	Red dyed bucktail, over which is gold crystal flash
Skirt:	Red crystal flash	Head:	Black
Body:	Orange long fiber crystal (Estaz,		

Gainesville, Florida, fly tier Dana Griffin says that a good fly for redfish must have "...flash and a color motif that wriggles through the red end of the visible spectrum (and) moves in a way suggestive of some bottom life form." Griffin also suggests fishing his impressionistic pattern on an outgoing tide at the mouth of tidal creeks flooding over oyster beds, where redfish often hang out to intercept food caught in the speeding current.

Tied by Tom Lentz

SANDFLEA

Hook:	Straight eye, standard length (usually size 1)		of the hook point
Tail:	Two small grizzly hackles	Body:	Rear half: Tan chenille
Eyes:	Painted white bead chain, mounted on the shank just ahead		Front half: Natural gray deer body hair, spun and trimmed as shown

Tom Lentz designed this pattern for a fly customer shortly after he "retired" and moved to Florida in the early 1980s. It is especially effective for pompano in the surf.

Tied by Jack Gartside

SANDHOPPER

| Hook: | Straight eye, standard length | Body: | Amber dyed fur, heavily dubbed |
| Back: | Three or four gold bead chain "eyes" secured on top of the hook shank | Legs: | Amber fur from the body, picked out |

Although sandhoppers (or sandfleas) are small and rarely exceed an inch in overall length, bonefish find them irresistible, and readily feed on them whenever they encounter them. This simple pattern, which is one of the best, was designed by Jack Gartside.

Tied by John Shewey

SURFPERCHER, RED

Hook:	Straight eye, standard length, tied hook point up	Wing:	Bright red marabou over which is red Flashabou
Tail:	Yellow marabou	Eyes:	Silver bead chain or chrome lead dumbbell eyes, secured with fluorescent red thread
Body:	Gold or red Diamond Braid		
Throat:	Yellow marabou		

This is one of the first flies that John Shewey tied expressly for surfperch. It dates back to the early 1980s when only he and a few friends were wading the Oregon coast in pursuit of this brawny "saltwater panfish." Surfperch, also known as "redtails" or "redtail surfperch," like to school and feed at shallow, sandy beaches. Once you locate fish, you'll probably be busy for a while.

A.J.'S SAND EEL

Hook: Straight eye, long shank
Tail: Sparse pearl crystal flash over which is white, violet, olive and tan craft fur. These materials are secured at the tail position, one end extending back to form the tail, the other end left long as it will be pulled forward to form the body
Eyes: Small bead chain with painted black pupils
Body: Butt ends of the tail pulled forward, overwrapped with pearl Mylar and covered with a thin coat of epoxy

A.J. Hand of Westport, Connecticut, developed this sand eel imitation "to fool the ultra-selective school stripers" that roam Connecticut's south shore which forms the northen border of Long Island Sound. Hand suggests that a light tippet and a "loop knot" will not restrict the movement of this fly.

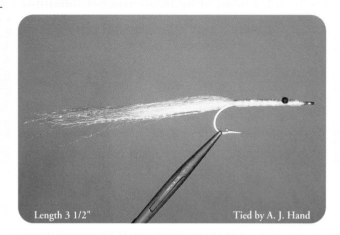

Length 3 1/2"   Tied by A. J. Hand

ANGUS, ORANGE & RED

Hook: Straight eye, standard length
Tail: Two pairs of hot orange hackles curving out
Underbody: Lead wire double wrapped over the front portion of the shank and overwrapped with orange floss
Hackle: Four or five hot orange marabou plumes palmered forward outside of which are several strands of pearl crystal flash
Collar: One or two red marabou plumes, wrapped
Head: Orange, red and black deer body hair, spun and trimmed as shown into a flat pointed wedge shape
Note: Although the original Angus was black, it is tied in a variety of color combinations for saltwater.

The Angus was developed by Eric Leiser, who is the author of many fly-tying books. Originally tied as a freshwater pattern for Alaskan rainbow trout, the Angus has been very effective as a saltwater fly as well.

Length 5"   Tied by Eric Leiser

BALAO

Hook: Straight eye, standard length
Wing: White FisHair over which is light blue and green FisHair and silver or gold Mylar on the sides. Pull tight and tie at the rear as shown with about a dozen wraps of olive thread, and trim
Head: Olive
Eyes: Black on yellow, with olive pupils
Note: When constructing this fly it's helpful to tie the white portion of the wing underneath the hook, to help the wing appear to be evenly spaced around the entire hook.

Frank Wentink, author of *Saltwater Fly Tying*, designed this fly to imitate the balao, or ballyhoo as it is frequently called. This common tropical saltwater forage fish travels in large schools and is found mostly inshore, often around grassy flats or reefs. Wentink tied this fly for barracuda, but just about everything including dorado, wahoo, sailfish and marlin keep an eye out for schools of balao.

Length 3"   Tied by Frank Wentink

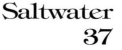

Length 7" Tied by Farrow Allen

BALLY HOO TAIL STREAMER

Hook: Straight eye, long or standard length
Wing: White over which is olive Ultra Hair or any other long synthetic hair, outside of which is silver Flashabou or Mylar
Eye: Plastic or painted eye of your choice
Nose: White with a painted olive top and a fluorescent red tip, coated with Epoxy
Note: Fan out the tail, tie it off with white thread and pinch it flat. Hold it in that position with a paper clasp, saturate the tail with Epoxy and cut a "V" notch as shown once dry.

This is a very realistic way of tying a balao imitation that Mike Praznovsky introduced in Robert Boyle and Dave Whitlock's 1978 *Second Fly-Tyers Almanac*. His technique is easily adapted to the imitation of a variety of baitfish.

Length 3" Tied by Ken Krohel

BEND BACK, KROHEL'S DEEP WATER

Hook: Straight eye, long shank, bend back style
Body: Gray chenille
Wing: Silver crystal flash over which is white, then black bucktail or FisHair topped by pearlescent purple crystal flash, flanked with two grizzly hackles curving in
Head: Red
Eyes: Painted white with black pupils

The bend back design is popular because the hook rides in a "point up" position which helps keep the fly weed free, and reduces snagging. This deep-water version has lead wraps under the chenille body, so the fly will sink rapidly. The bend back is more a style than it is a specific fly pattern, and you can adapt it to a great number of flies.

Length 3" Tied by Chuck Scates

BEND BACK, HOT BUTT

Hook: Straight eye, standard length, bend back style
Butt: Fluorescent pink chenille
Body: Fluorescent white chenille
Wing: Two or four white hackles over which is pearl crystal flash over which is sparse white bucktail topped by peacock herl

Chuck Scates operates the Shallow Water Guide Service in south Texas where he specializes in fishing the flats for redfish and seatrout. This fly is one of his favorites; it is fished below the floating weeds, but above the flats grass.

BLOSSOM, ORANGE

Hook: Straight eye, standard length
Wing: Orange marabou, tied full
Head: Orange chenille

This old, yet simple and effective style of streamer developed from the collaborative efforts of several New Jersey shore anglers including Mark Sosin and George Cornish. It can be tied in a variety of colors including yellow (Lemon Blossom), white (Apple Blossom) and pink (Cherry Blossom).

Length 3 1/2"   Tied by Farrow Allen

BLUEFISH STREAMER

Hook: Straight eye, long shank
Wing: White bucktail outside of which is pearl Flashabou and over which is white Ultra Hair and blue Ultra Hair, all topped by peacock herl
Throat: Fluff from the base of a hackle dyed red
Eyes: Silver bead chain or lead
Head: Fluorescent red, coated with epoxy
Note: This fly may be tied in any colors that match local baitfish.

Because bluefish are voracious feeders and their teeth are razor sharp, it's helpful to tie your bluefish flies keeping most of the materials as far away from the leader as possible. It's always a good idea to use a steel leader when blues are around, but if the hook shank is long enough your leader should be safe for a while.

Length 6"   Tied by Farrow Allen

BOB'S SILICLONE BUCKTAIL

Hook: Straight eye, standard length
Wing: Purple bucktail
Wool head: Purple lamb's wool spun and trimmed to shape, overwrapped with purple crystal chenille
Head: Clear silicone rubber spread over the wool head, shaped as shown and sprinkled with glitter flakes
Eyes: Peel-off, stick-on prismatic eyes
Note: After applying the eyes and glitter flakes add a final coat of silicone rubber to the head.

An easy to tie all-purpose surface minnow imitation that is a part of Bob Popovics' Siliclone series. It can be tied in any color desired.

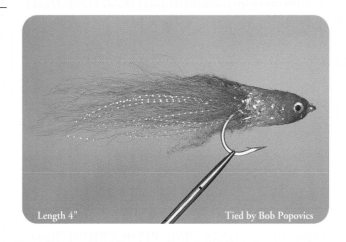

Length 4"   Tied by Bob Popovics

Length 6"   Tied by Bob Popovics

BOB'S SILICLONE MULLET

Hook: Straight eye, standard length
Wing: Yellow bucktail over which are half a dozen or more yellow hackles curving in, with a final pair on top tied flat and curving down
Collar: Yellow lamb's wool
Wool head: Yellow lamb's wool spun and trimmed to shape
Head: Clear silicone rubber spread over the wool head, shaped as shown and sprinkled with glitter flakes
Eyes: Peel-off, stick-on prismatic eyes
Note: After applying the eyes and glitter flakes add a final coat of silicone rubber to the head.

This is one of Bob Popovics "full dress" Siliclone flies "that presents a wide profile and a large cylindrical shape . . . a top rider with good action."

Length 4"   Tied by Phil Chapman

BOCA GRANDE TARPON SAND PERCH
EXPRESS

Hook: Straight eye, standard length
Wing: Pearl Flashabou surrounded by blue bucktail, outside of which are six grizzly hackles, three on each side, over which is purple Flashabou
Collar: Rusty orange deer body hair
Head: Bands of rusty orange, gray and blue deer body hair stacked over gray deer body hair, trimmed as shown, close on the bottom and flat on the sides
Eyes: Oversize solid plastic

Developed in the mid 1980s by Capt. Phil Chapman of Lakeland, Florida, "for beach-running schools of tarpon in the Boca Grande Pass area." The sand perch, or squirrelfish as it is locally known, is a favorite forage fish for tarpon in this area.

Length 4"   Tied by Jamie Dickinson

BROOKS BLONDE, ARGENTINE

Hook: Straight eye, standard length
Tail: White bucktail
Body: Flat silver Mylar tinsel
Wing: Light blue bucktail
Head: Blue

The Blondes were introduced for saltwater fishing by Joe Brooks around the early 1960s. Brooks considered the Platinum Blonde (white), the Honey Blonde (yellow), and the Strawberry Blonde (orange and red) in sizes 1/0 to 4/0 to be "the best strike-bringers." The "tail" is tied long and is considered to be the lower part of the wing, and this style renders a virtually foul-proof fly. A few strands of modern, flashy synthetic wing material are often included when tying this pattern today.

CAPE COD EEL #1

Hook: Straight eye, standard length
Wing: A pair of natural brown schlappen hackles over which are two pairs of natural black schlappen hackles
Collar: Mixed brown and natural black schlappen hackles wound together
Eyes: Chrome lead dumbbell eyes secured with black thread

Michael Arritt who ties flies commercially on Cape Cod at East Falmouth, Massachusetts, ties this, as well as a dun and grizzly variation, for striped bass. Fishing mostly at night, using one of his eels and a full sinking line, Arritt and others have landed many fish over 40 lbs.

Length 8" Tied by Michael Arritt

CARY'S MINNOW, CRYSTAL FLASH

Hook: Straight eye, long shank
Underbody: White chenille
Throat: Red marabou
Eyes: Solid plastic
Body and tail: Pearl crystal flash over which is peacock crystal flash topped by black crystal flash. The tail is tied off with olive thread as well as the head
Weedguard: Monofilament

Brooks Bouldin of the Angler's Edge in Houston asked Cary Marcus to design an effective fly to imitate a Mud Minnow, a favorite forage of the local flounder. This is the fly, and Bouldin says that it's lived up to his greatest expectations. He reports that it's not easy to tie, but it's well worth the effort.

Length 2" Tied by Angler's Edge

CAVE'S RATTLIN' MINNOW

Hook: Straight eye, long shank, bend back style
Underbody: Glass, plastic or metal rattle chamber secured to the shank opposite the bend; over the rattle attach a piece of flat twist-on lead or similar to insure that the fly swims with the hook point up (tied with the hook point down, the lead need not be used)
Body: Pearlescent Mylar tubing, secured at the rear of the fly with white thread, leaving a short length of mylar unravelled to form a tail
Wing: A large bunch of white bucktail over which are a few strands of pearl crystal flash over which is black bucktail
Cheeks: Red Flashabou, short
Head: Black with painted yellow eyes with black pupils

Developed in the early 1980s by author and Florida fly fishing guide Jon Cave. (see Cave's Tarpon Rattler) "According to studies," says Cave "fish can hear at lower decibel levels than humans and are able to detect even slight disturbances and displacements of water." In certain situations the added attraction of sound can be helpful in getting a fish's attention.

Length 3" Tied by Jon Cave

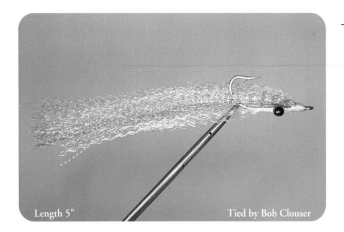

Length 5" Tied by Bob Clouser

CLOUSER DEEP MINNOW (ULTRA) BALLYHOO

Hook: Straight eye, standard length
Eyes: Lead dumbbell eyes secured on top of the hook with white thread, painted red with black pupils
Throat: Polar bear Ultra Hair
Wing: Green Ultra Hair over which is a long and a short bunch of pearl crystal flash topped by light blue Ultra Hair

Bob Clouser is a guide and a fly shop owner from Middletown, Pennsylvania, who designed the Deep Minnow for smallmouth bass. Like many good baitfish imitations, its application goes far beyond the point of origin. This is his representation of the important ballyhoo (balao). Early Deep Minnows were dressed with bucktail; when Ultra Hair became available, Clouser began using this translucent synthetic hair. The orientation of Clouser Deep Minnows is with the hook point up.

Length 5" Tied by Bob Clouser

CLOUSER DEEP MINNOW, GIZZARD SHAD

Hook: Straight eye, standard length
Eyes: Lead dumbbell eyes secured on top of the hook with gray thread, painted red with black pupils
Throat: White bucktail
Wing: Silver crystal flash and silver Flashabou over which is gray bucktail topped with a short section of red bucktail

Clouser first tied the Gizzard Shad for striped bass fishing on the lower Susquehanna River flats. The success of this design has made it one of the most important baitfish imitations to have been developed.

Length 5" Tied by Bob Clouser

CLOUSER HALF & HALF

Hook: Straight eye, standard length
Eyes: Lead dumbbell eyes secured on top of the hook with light blue thread, painted red with black pupils
Rear wing: Six to eight white hackles surrounded by a bunch of long silver Flashabou, over which is short silver Flashabou, and a short bunch of light blue bucktail below
Front wing: Two short sections of light blue bucktail, one tied in behind the eyes and the other in front of the eyes

Bob Clouser tied this amalgamated minnow imitation, the rear part of which is basically a Lefty's Deceiver and the front part a Clouser Deep Minnow. Clouser's intent was to imitate ". . . a twisting, diving bright-sided minnow."

CREASE FLY MINNOW

Hook: Straight eye, long shank
Tail: Blue-gray bucktail over pearl crystal flash, topped with sparse olive-brown bucktail over which is peacock crystal flash
Body: Trim a sheet of "Live body" foam to shape as shown, fold and glue with a heavy duty CA cement and pinch together on the bottom until securely fastened on the hook shank. Once you've pinched and squeezed the body material into the shape you like, place several drops of CA cement inside the creased body and carefully spray inside with an accelerant; color as desired
Eyes: Peel-off, stick-on prismatic eyes
Note: After the body has been colored, and the eyes have been applied, coat the entire body with epoxy.

Joe Blados of Southold, Long Island (New York), uses this body technique to make all kinds of realistic minnows, crabs and squid.

Length 4" Tied by Joe Blados

CURVE & DIVE STREAMER

Hook: Straight eye, standard length
Body: Gold Mylar tubing, secured with red thread
Eyes: Lead, painted white with black pupils
Wing: A single yellow-dyed cock ringneck pheasant shoulder feather (with a slightly twisted stem) trimmed and tied flat, curving down "at a slight angle so that the stem extends to one side of the hook shank and then curves back to the opposite side." Over this are two dyed-yellow ringneck pheasant blood feathers, tied flat
Head: Red thread wrapped around the lead eyes

Corbett Davis of Gulf Breeze, Florida, spent a lot of time developing this pattern for seatrout in salt or brackish water. It is most effective when the Gulf waters are cool, and seatrout are down six to twelve feet. Davis writes, "For best results I recommend a swim-and-jig retrieve, slow at first, and then progressively faster as necessary."

Length 2" Tied by Corbett Davis

DAHLBERG DIVER

Hook: Straight eye, standard length
Tail: Gold Flashabou over which are several light ginger variant hackles and a short bunch of cream and tan marabou
Collar: Golden-tan deer body hair over the top and sides only
Head and diving collar: Golden-tan deer body hair spun and clipped to shape as shown and cemented on the bottom

Developed by Larry Dahlberg to dive, swim and resurface. Variations of the Dahlberg Diver can be effectively fished inshore, casting to redfish, seatrout, striped bass, bluefish and tarpon in calm water. Dahlberg often ties his saltwater flies on freshwater hooks. He says that he usually loses them, or they are destroyed by fish, before they get a chance to rust.

Length 4" Tied by Larry Dahlberg

Length 3 1/2"   Tied by David Olson

DEER HAIR DECEIVER

Hook: Straight eye, long shank
Wing: Yellow bucktail outside of which are two light fluorescent green hackles curving inward and veiled with several strands of chartreuse crystal flash
Skirt: Fluorescent green deer body hair
Body: Fluorescent light green deer body hair, spun and trimmed in a tapered cylinder as shown
Collar: Sparse fluorescent light green hackle

David Olson, who manages the fishing department at The Outdoor Shop in Tallahassee, Florida, developed this highly successful snook, redfish and seatrout fly in the early 1980s. He ties it in several color variations: pink with a grizzly wing and hackle; and white with a grizzly wing and red hackle. Olson says that "... day or night the green is the best ... it should be fished in the surface film where it creates a wake."

Length 2 1/2"   Tied by Joe Butorac

ELECTRIC MINNOW

Hook: Straight eye, long shank, offset bend
Underbody: From a plastic coffee can lid or similar, cut a right and a left minnow form, using serrated scissors, because the edge left by serrated scissors is rough and holds the thread wraps. Secure both sides to the hook shank (over a base of yarn or chenille)
Body: Peacock crystal flash over unravelled, combed-out pearl Mylar tubing, pulled over the plastic form and secured at the rear with transparent sewing thread
Tail: Peacock crystal flash over pearl Mylar tubing, trimmed as shown
Eyes: Black paint
Note: After eyes have been painted, coat the entire body with epoxy. By unravelling the Mylar tubing and combing it out, the size of the fly is no longer limited by the diameter of the Mylar tubing you're able to find. "You can fish side by side with Mirror-Lure and Rapala fishermen with equal results," says the developer, Joe Butorac, of Arlington, Washington.

Length 3"   Tied by Don Avondolio

EPOXY SILVERSIDES

Hook: Straight eye, long shank
Tail: Fine white bucktail with shorter silver crystal flash on top
Body: Silver braided Mylar tinsel
Wing: Fine white bucktail over which are optional strands of olive bucktail extending to the end of the tail
Throat: Wraps of red thread; or gill plates drawn with a red marking pen after the head has been epoxied
Head: Silver braided Mylar tinsel
Eyes: Peel-off, stick-on prismatic eyes
Note: Coat the entire head with epoxy after the eyes have been applied.

The Atlantic silversides is a major food source for striped bass and bluefish throughout most of the northern portion of the Atlantic coast. Don Avondolio, a long time member of the Salty Flyrodders of New York, developed this pattern for his home waters of Long Island Sound.

ERIC'S BABY BUNKER

Hook: Straight eye, standard length

Wing: Mixed pearl and silver crystal flash, on each side of which is one white marabou plume, outside of which are a few more strands of pearl crystal flash

Collar: Fine white bucktail tied in at the hook eye, extending beyond the bend of the hook, over which is rainbow crystal flash and peacock herl

Head: Clear silicone rubber spread over the collar, squeezed flat and sprinkled with glitter flakes

Eyes: Peel-off, stick-on prismatic eyes

Note: After applying the eyes and glitter flakes add a thin coat of silicone rubber over the head.

Eric Peterson's Baby Bunker was developed for striped bass and bluefish and can be tied to imitate a host of flat-sided baitfish

Length 4"   Tied by Eric Peterson

ERIC'S FLOATING SAND EEL

Hook: Straight eye, standard length

Tail: Black craft fur over which is black crystal flash or Twinkle, cemented into a slit made in the rear half of the body

Body: Section of round, black, closed cell foam, mounted on the hook

Eyes: Painted silver with black pupils

When striped bass or bluefish are charging through schools of sand eels, it is often effective to fish along the edges with a floating imitation that isn't obscured by the mass of the school. Also, in quiet tidal pools and slow moving creeks, small floating imitations like this one can bring exciting results.

Length 4"   Tied by Eric Peterson

ERIC'S SAND EEL

Hook: Straight eye, long shank

Tail: Sparse white craft fur over which is very sparse light olive, lavender and tan craft fur

Underbody: Craft fur from the tail is pulled forward over the hook shank and secured at the head position. Use care to maintain the color separation

Eye: Peel-off, stick-on prismatic eyes, applied to the underbody

Body: Clear monofilament coated with epoxy

Throughout the season sand eels are abundant along sandy beaches and tidal creeks where hungry stripers frequently chase them right into the shore - especially at daybreak and at dusk. Because of the sand eels' small size, and their proximity to shore, imitations are appealing to the wading angler.

Length 4"   Tied by Eric Peterson

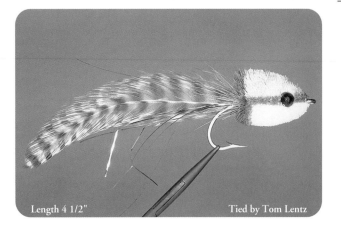

Length 4 1/2"   Tied by Tom Lentz

FINGER MULLET

Hook: Straight eye, standard length
Wing: Two grizzly hackles and sparse silver, olive and gold Flashabou on the sides
Collar: Natural deer body hair
Eyes: Bead chain, painted black
Head: A band of natural gray deer body hair (butt ends of the collar), white deer body hair spun and trimmed as shown. A red throat, a green lateral stripe, and a pale gray top to the head are applied with waterproof marking pens

The Finger Mullet is popular as a tarpon fly. Mullet are abundant along the entire east coast and provide forage for many inshore gamefish; at one time or another practically everything feeds on mullet. Tom Lentz tied this pattern for us but credits the idea to Bill Catherwood (See Catherwood's Herring, Hair Head).

Length 4"   Tied by Paul Sequira

FLASHYEEL

Hook: Straight eye, long shank
Tail: White bucktail over which are longer narrow white hackles flanked by pearl crystal flash as long as the bucktail
Body: Pearl crystal chenille
Wing: Olive bucktail over which is peacock herl, tied in at the head, pulled over the body like a shellback and secured at the tail as shown
Eyes: Peel-off, stick-on prismatic eyes
Head: White thread, colored dark green on top and thickly coated with cement

Originated for striped bass and bluefish by Paul Sequira, who fishes in New York's Long Island Sound. His Flashyeel is a good working imitation of the common "sand eel," and it can be modified by color and size to imitate other small baitfish.

Length 3"   Tied by Carl Hanson

GLASS MINNOW, HANSON'S

Hook: Straight eye, standard length
Wing: White bucktail over which is blue bucktail
Underbody: After tying in the white bucktail, wrap over it with silver Mylar tinsel to the bend of the hook and back. Tie in the blue bucktail and build up the head with red thread
Overbody: 12 lb. to 20 lb. clear monofilament binding down the blue bucktail wing over the silver Mylar body, whip finished

Carl Hanson tied his original Glass Minnow about 1950. Chico Fernandez, recognizing the value of Hanson's design, created some variations which became popular. (see the Glass Minnow on page 47) Hanson himself has modified his original design over the years and currently ties the Glass Minnow on a bend back hook.

GLASS MINNOW

Hook: Straight eye, standard length
Body: Flat silver tinsel overwrapped with clear 12 lb. to 20 lb. monofilament (using a razor blade, trim the monofilament to a fine tapered point to avoid a bulge at the tie in point)
Wing: White FisHair over which is silver Flashabou
Head: White with painted yellow eyes with black pupils, with several wraps of fluorescent red thread at the rear
Note: Other popular variations include brown hair over white and green hair over yellow or white. The body overwrap may also be of clear Swannundaze or V-Wrap.

Saltwater expert Chico Fernandez, of Miami, ties his Glass Minnows in many different colors. "Glass minnow" is the common name applied to a widely mixed group of nearly transparent, thin-bodied minnows that are frequently encountered in saltwater.

Length 3"   Tied by Umpqua Feather Merchants

HARE-O-SHIMA SNOOK FLY

Hook: Straight eye, standard length
Tail: White bucktail over which is pearl crystal flash flanked by two grizzly hackles, curving out, topped with a white rabbit-fur strip which is topped with sparse pearl Flashabou
Body: Rear ½: Wrapped white rabbit-fur strip, over which are a few long peacock herls
        Front ½: Wrapped red rabbit-fur strip
Weedguard: Stainless steel wire

This is one of Phil Chapman's early snook flies which he introduced in 1980 for fishing in the heaviest mangrove cover where snook love to hide. Chapman, a guide and Florida State fishery biologist, describes the Hare-O-Shima as a "versatile and durable fly that seldom fouls."

Length 4"   Tied by Phil Chapman

HERRING, HAIR HEAD

Hook: Straight eye, standard length
Underwing: A white, light pink, light blue and white marabou feather, attached in this order, bottom to top. You want to choose plumes with fairly rigid stems; these will help to support the wing and keep it from wrapping around the hook.
Wing: On each side a set of two light blue hackles outside of which are two pearl gray hackles, tied in so the base fluff is showing
Sides: Pink, light blue and dark blue crystal flash
Head: White and light blue deer body hair, spun and trimmed as shown
Eyes: Solid glass

This is Bill Catherwood's original dressing of the Hair Head Herring, except that he now uses crystal flash to replace the original Emu-plume sides. Catherwood, of Tewksbury, Massachusetts, was the first tier that we know of who used a clipped deer hair head on a saltwater fly.

Length 7"   Tied by Bill Catherwood

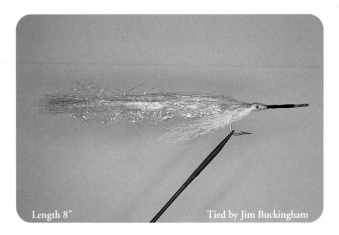

Length 8"   Tied by Jim Buckingham

JIM BUCK BALLYHOO

Hook: Straight eye, long shank
Wing: Pearl braided Mylar threaded over the hook (unravelled as a final step after the fly has been completed), green FisHair over which is blue FisHair
Throat: White bucktail
Head: Fluorescent green or yellow
Eyes: Peel off, stick on fluorescent green with black pupils
Nose: Black thread with a fluorescent rose tip
Note: Cover the head, eyes and nose with a thin coat of epoxy.

This is Jim Buckingham's basic ballyhoo imitation. His original fly, named the "Jim Buck" by Stu Apte, dates back to the 1960s and was tied with a wing of polar bear hair and silver Mylar. An offshore variation is tied the same but uses a short spun-deer-hair collar that's tied on before the wing and pushes the wing up, giving the impression of a much bigger fly.

Length 8"   Tied by Bob Popovics

KEEL EEL

Hook: Straight eye, long shank with the front part bent in the typical "bend back" style
(Before tying the wing, wrap flat gold Mylar over the bent-up portion of the hook where the epoxied head will be)
Wing: Short Polar Bear Ultra Hair over which is long dark brown Ultra Hair
Head: Epoxy saturating the very front part of the wing
Eyes: Peel-off, stick-on prismatic yellow eyes with black pupils
Gills and mouth: Painted on with a red marking pen
Note: After the eyes and mouth have been applied add a final light coat of epoxy over the entire head.

This is Bob Popovics' imitation of an American Eel which is a favorite bait for big, nocturnal striped bass. Tied "bend back" style, this fly is nearly weedless.

Length 4"   Tied by Farrow Allen

LEFTY'S BIG-EYE DECEIVER

Hook: Straight eye, standard length
Wing: Six to ten white saddle hackles, curving together
Body: Tying thread, wound forward
Collar: Two bunches of white bucktail on each side, extending beyond the hook point
Throat: Red hair or fur
Topping: Peacock herl
Cheeks: Mallard breast treated with flexible cement and trimmed to shape
Eyes: Painted yellow with black pupils
Head: Red

The Big-Eye Deceiver can be tied large or small in as many color variations as needed to match a a wide range of forage fish. Kreh says "The Deceiver isn't a precise pattern, it's a style or type of fly - it can be tied in many colors and various lengths. . ."

LEFTY'S DECEIVER, OLIVE

Hook: Straight eye, standard length
Wing: Six to ten matched white saddles outside of which, along each side, is a grizzly hackle dyed pale olive and a few strands of pearl or olive crystal flash or Flashabou
Body: Tying thread, wound forward, in this case fluorescent green
Collar: Two bunches of white bucktail, one applied on each side, extending well beyond the the hook point
Throat: Red crystal flash
Topping: Peacock herl
Head: Green crystal flash, epoxy coated. Eyes optional

Lefty Kreh developed the Deceiver in the 1960s for striped bass fishing around the Chesapeake Bay. Since then there's hardly been a gamefish in salt- or freshwater that hasn't fallen prey to a Deceiver. The fly is popular because it meets several critical design imperatives: it casts well, rarely fouls, and can be modified to imitate any type baitfish. The Deceiver may be the best saltwater streamer yet designed.

Length 4" Tied by Lefty Kreh

LIVEBODY SLIDER

Hook: Straight eye, long shank
Tail: White bucktail over which is fluorescent green bucktail, olive, copper and metallic blue Flashabou
Skirt: Fluorescent green hackle
Underbody: Narrow cylinder of floating (Live body) foam, slit and secured to the hook shank
Overbody: Pearl braided Mylar, pulled over the foam underbody and secured front and back with a neutral thread; colored green on top with a marking pen
Eyes: Peel-off, stick-on eyes, prismatic
Note: After the eyes have been placed, coat entire body with epoxy.

This pattern was designed by Bruce Cleveland of Brooklyn, New York, for striped bass and bluefish. It has also proved attractive to other surface feeders, particularly barracuda. Fished on the surface, the Livebody Slider dives, skips and creates an enticing wake as it's retrieved.

Length 5" Tied by Bruce Cleveland

LOVING BASS FLY

Hook: Straight eye, standard length
Wing: White bucktail
Collar: Red hackle
Head: Black

This fly dates back to the 1920s when it was developed by Tom Loving for striped bass fishing in the Chesapeake Bay area. Although you won't find this fly in modern catalogs, if you were to tie a few and throw them at a bass, snook, or even a tarpon, you know what would probably happen.

Length 3 1/2" Tied by Dick Stewart

Length 3"   Tied by Ken Krohel

MACK ATTACK

Hook: Straight eye, long shank, fine wire
Underbody: A minnow-shaped form constructed of hot glue or plastic
Body: Silver braided Mylar pulled over the underbody. Over this is pearl crystal flash, green Ultra Hair with peacock crystal flash on top. These components are secured with olive thread at both the front and rear, with excess materials extending back to form the tail. The body is coated with several applications of epoxy.
Lateral line: Painted fluorescent green stripe
Eye: Painted white with black pupils
Note: A final coat of epoxy is applied after the eyes and lateral line have been painted.

Ken Krohel designed this fly to imitate "the thin profile of a small Spanish sardine." He believes the bright fluorescent green lateral stripe helps a mackerel to pick his fly out of the crowd.

Length 5"   Tied by Tim Borski

MANGROVE GHOST

Hook: Straight eye, standard length
Wing: A bunch of white craft fur, streamer hair or fine bucktail, over which are ten or more white saddle hackles curving in, with several strands of pearl crystal flash on top
Collar: White webby barbs from the butt ends of a couple of white saddle hackles
Eyes: Melted monofilament, secured across the hook shank forming a wide head
Head: Both the hook shank and the stem of the eyes are wrapped with gold tinsel. A large, wide head is formed with epoxy

Tim Borski designed this fly to be thrown at snook hiding deep in heavy mangrove cover; thus it is usually tied with a monofilament weedguard.

Length 4"   Tied by Jamie Dickinson

McNALLY SMELT

Hook: Straight eye, standard length
Body: Flat silver tinsel
Wing: White bucktail over which is peacock herl
Cheeks: Mallard breast or flank feather
Head: White

An early saltwater streamer that Tom McNally tied in the general shape and basic color of many baitfish. McNally has spent most of his life working as an outdoor writer.

MIDNIGHT MAGIC

Hook: Straight eye, standard length
Wing: Black bucktail, applied like a collar, peacock herl on top and purple crystal flash on the sides
Eyes: Peel-off, stick-on prismatic eyes
Head: Black with a red band behind the eyes, coated with cement or epoxy

Jaiem Fleischmann lives in Jackson Heights and fishes Long Island Sound, New York. He describes this pattern as a "simple but incredibly effective striped bass fly." As the name implies, he developed it primarily for night fishing, particularly during the early season when small baitfish are abundant inshore.

Length 3"   Tied by Jaiem Fleishmann

MONO GLASS MINNOW

Hook: Straight eye, long shank
Underbody: Lead wire, over which is white chenille
Wing: A few strands of pearl crystal flash over which is a large bunch of white FisHair over which is a smaller bunch of fluorescent green FisHair over which is a smaller bunch of blue FisHair, all trimmed into a tapered head and cut flat in back
Topping: Peacock crystal flash tied in at the head, doubled back over the wing and tied down with red thread ⅓ way back on the body
Eyes: Peel-off, stick-on prismatic eyes
Overbody: 40 lb. monofilament, snelled over the body, being careful to keep the body and wing straight. Once wrapped, tighten with pliers. The tag end will serve as a shock tippet.

Designed by John Bottko of Jacksonville, Florida, the durable Mono Glass Minnow is an excellent baitfish imitation. Bottko says it's well proven on Spanish mackerel, jack crevalle, bluefish, ladyfish and bonita.

Length 3 1/2"   Tied by John Bottko

MYSTERY FLY, TAN

Hook: Straight eye, standard length or short shank
Tail: Two tan-dyed butts from a grizzly hen hackle, tied flat on top and curving down. The hackle tips are cut away
Underbody: About four beads of a bead chain, secured along the top of the hook
Body: As many tan-dyed hen grizzly hackle butts (or soft saddle hackle butts or blood marabou feathers) as needed to palmer the length of the hook shank

Jack Gartside named this fly the "Mystery Fly, because I have no idea why it works, but it does, and sometimes when no other fly will take a tarpon ... it arouses a curiosity in otherwise reluctant fish." Gartside ties it in other colors, but says tan is the one they bite the best.

Length 3"   Tied by Jack Gartside

Length 3"   Tied by Jack Montague

MYSTERY MINNOW

Hook: Straight eye, long shank
Tail: White over which is brown craft fur, and gold Flashabou (leave enough Flashabou to pull forward over the body later)
Underbody: A strip of prismatic tape, folded over the shank and trimmed in the shape of a minnow
Body: Epoxy, applied in two stages
Back: The balance of the gold crystal flash pulled forward over the first epoxy coat
Gills and lateral line: Black marking pen
Eyes: Red sequins with painted black pupils (see Montague's Epoxy Permit)

A flashy translucent minnow imitation that Jack Montague developed during the mid 1980s as an alternative to traditional hairwing or featherwing streamers.

NEEDLEFISH

Hook: Straight eye, long shank
Underwing: White, pearl gray, pink, Rit "sea foam" green, and medium blue marabou tied in this order
Wing: Four pale grayish blue-green hackles, outside of which are "sea foam" green and pearl gray hackles
Eyes: Amber glass
Nose: Green

Bill Catherwood, a long time commercial fly tier from Tewksbury, Massachusetts, developed his version of a needlefish in the late 1950s. Catherwood was probably the first tier to tie in this style, with the wing placed above the hook point and nothing in front but head and eyes. This design results in a good needlefish imitation and it also helps eliminate those problems caused by the wing wrapping itself around the hook.

Length 5"   Tied by Bill Catherwood

Length 8"   Tied by Jack Montague

NEEDLEFISH

Hook: Straight eye, long shank
Wing: White bucktail outside of which are two wide, webby badger hackles and two shorter ones, over which is gold Flashabou
Collar: White craft fur on the lower ¾ of the fly, olive craft fur on top ¼, peacock herl over
Head and nose: Built up, painted as shown and coated with epoxy
Eyes: Painted white with black pupils and coated with epoxy

"Needlefish," says Montague, "are very agile swimmers and sometimes difficult for snook to catch, except when the needlefish themselves are preoccupied with feeding." To imitate a feeding needlefish, Montague runs a small Colorado spinner on his leader, directly ahead of the fly. "To a hungry snook this looks like a needlefish with a minnow in its mouth and draws more strikes."

NIGHT SNOOK FLY

Hook: Straight eye, standard length
Tail: Pearl Flashabou
Wings: Pearl Flashabou, applied in two bunches: one about midway on the shank, the other at the head
Body: White tying thread
Head: White with painted black eyes and yellow pupils
Weedguard: Stainless steel wire, size #5

Designed by Jim Grace for snook fishing at night around lighted piers and bridges. This fly is most effective when tied in smaller sizes.

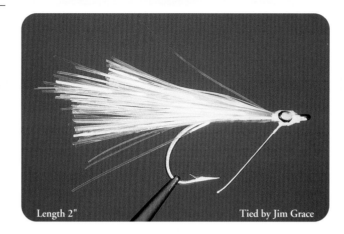

Length 2"   Tied by Jim Grace

PEACOCK SWORD DECEIVER

Hook: Straight eye, long shank
Body: Pearl braided Mylar or Flashabou Minnow Body, pulled over the shank and unravelled in back
Wing: White bucktail over which is crystal flash, pink bucktail and purple bucktail, topped with the tip of a peacock sword feather
Head: White thread, built up and wrapped with pearl crystal flash and coated with epoxy
Eyes: Peel-off, stick-on prismatic eyes

Lenny Moffo ties this streamer in several colors, although all feature the peacock sword topping. It's a good looking fly which is tied in the style of the Streaker (which see).

Length 4"   Tied by Lenny Moffo

PERCY'S SAND EEL

Hook: Straight eye, standard or long shank
Tail: Fluorescent green FisHair
Body: Telephone cable wire in a color that compliments the color of the tail, ribbed with fine oval silver tinsel
Note: Within a trunk of telephone cable there are numerous wires with different colors of insulation, all of which will produce slightly weighted bodies for this fly.

This sand eel was developed by the Percy Tackle Company of Portland, Maine, after it was taken over by Peter Sang in 1972. The original owner, Gardiner Percy, began the company in the 1800s, and supplied flies throughout New England.

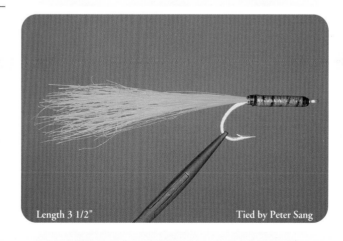

Length 3 1/2"   Tied by Peter Sang

Length 3" Tied by Dave Johnson

PETTI-COAT STREAMER

Hook: Straight eye, standard length
Tail: White FisHair
Underbody: Flat silver Mylar tinsel
Body: 15 lb. clear monofilament, epoxy coated
Wing: White marabou barbs, trimmed from the stem, placed in a spinning (dubbing) loop, spun and wrapped like a long collar
Topping: Light blue crystal flash (optional)
Eyes: Silver bead chain, secured with white thread

Developed as a freshwater fly in 1975 by Dave Johnson, a fly tier now living in Decatur, Alabama, this saltwater version has accounted for tarpon, bones, reds and specks.

Length 2" Tied by Phillip Beckett

PHILLIP BECKETT'S PINFISH

Hook: Straight eye, standard length
Body: Silver braided Mylar, slipped over the hook shank and secured at the rear with white thread
Tail: Unravelled silver braided Mylar
Throat: White bucktail
Wing: White bucktail over which is light blue bucktail over which is green bucktail and pearl crystal flash
Cheeks: Barred mallard or teal flank feathers, covering most of the wing
Eyes: Small hollow plastic, cemented to the cheeks

This fly was developed in 1978 by Phillip Beckett of Melbourne, Florida, for fishing for baby tarpon while exploring the creeks and canals of southern Florida.

Length 2 1/2" Tied by Tom Piccolo

PIC-A-BOMBER

Hook: Straight eye, standard length
Tail: Fluorescent green marabou and chartreuse crystal flash
Body: Fluorescent green chenille
Body hackle: Fluorescent green, palmered
Eyes: Lead dumbbell eyes, painted yellow with black pupils, tied on the top of the hook shank
Collar: Fluorescent green hackle
Head: Fluorescent green with a red stripe

The Pic-A-Bomber is a weighted, deep-running saltwater Woolly Bugger which, along with an unweighted version known as a Pic-A-Bugger, was originated by Tom Piccolo of the Sportsman's Den of Greenwich, Connecticut, on the northern shore of Long Island Sound. Both variations have been effective for striped bass. Further south, bonefish, small tarpon, snook and the occasional permit have also fallen for these flies.

PICK FLY, HERRING

Hook: Straight eye, standard length
Underbody-Rear: Cut off the back end of a large, flat, wood toothpick and secure it on the top rear ½ of the hook so it tapers toward the eye
Tail: Long white bucktail evenly distributed over toothpick foundation, with a few strands each of pearl, silver and very sparse lime Flashabou on each side
Body: Braided silver Mylar over the rear half of the shank only
Under body-Front: 3 pieces of toothpick (2 on top, 1 on bottom) flattened on the front end to form a steeply tapered wedge shaped head
Throat: White bucktail distributed over the bottom toothpick
Wing: White bucktail evenly distributed and flared over the top toothpick foundation, over which is a small bunch of light blue bucktail topped by dark blue bucktail
Head: White with a painted stripe of dark blue on top
Eye: Painted black

Jim DiGregorio's fly looks big, but casts easily since it has very little bulk.

Length 5"   Tied by Jim DiGregorio

PICKPOCKET

Hook: Straight eye, standard length
Tail: White bucktail over which is green bucktail
Body: Braided silver Mylar tinsel or Poly Flash, wrapped
Wing: Two olive hackles outside of which are 2 grizzly hackles dyed purple, followed by 2 plain grizzly hackles
Cheeks: Barred teal flank
Collar: Very soft white hackle
Head: Fluorescent red
Eyes: Painted yellow with black pupils

Mike Martinek, from Stoneham, Massachusetts, originated the Pickpocket in 1968 for school stripers in Cape Cod Bay. Over the years it has been effective for bluefish and large bass as well. Although it resembles a tinker mackerel, a major forage in the northeast, the Pickpocket has taken a variety of fish in southern waters, including many tarpon.

Length 5"   Tied by Mike Martinek

POPE

Hook: Straight eye, standard length
Wing: Tied at the rear of the hook, above the barb: polar bear or substitute dyed a pale shade of rosy-salmon with red tips, over which is orange crystal flash and a slightly longer black rabbit fur strip
Body: Fluorescent red thread, very short
Collar: Polar bear or substitute, dyed rosy-salmon with red tips, tied mostly on top
Head: Fluorescent red thread
Weedguard: Stainless steel wire, size #5

The Pope is one of Captain Jim Grace's all-time favorite snook flies. He based his design on a fly from another Florida guide, Phil Chapman, whose flies are also included in this book. The fly is named the Pope because it's "infallible."

Length 3"   Tied by Jim Grace

Length 5"   Tied by Bob Popovics

RABBIT CANDY

Hook: Straight eye, standard length
Tail support: A loop of stiff monofilament
Tail: Fluorescent green rabbit fur strip
Body: Silver Mylar tubing wrapped around the hook shank veiled by
         fluorescent green crystal hair that is saturated with epoxy mixed
         with sparkle flakes
Eyes: Peel-off, stick-on prismatic eyes, fluorescent green
Throat: Painted red with a marking pen
Note: After the eyes and mouth have been applied, add a final light
         coat of epoxy over the entire body.

Bob Popovics says that this is his "most effective Candy for striped
bass . . . you can't be without this one."

Length 3 1/2"   Tied by Chuck Scates

RED NOSE MUD MINNOW

Hook: Straight eye, standard length
Wing: White bucktail over which is green Flashabou. On each side are
         two medium blue saddle hackles flanked by two yellow saddle
         hackles
Collar: Natural deer body hair
Head: Spun natural deer body hair with red deer body hair for the nose,
         spun and clipped to shape as shown
Eyes: Hollow plastic

Chuck Scates developed this fly as a surface slider for seatrout and redfish
on the South Texas flats, where he operates a guide service. It's a mud
minnow (finger mullet) imitation that's useful when hungry reds are on
shallow grass flats chasing schools of bait right up to the shore.

Length 8"   Tied by Bill Peabody

RHODY FLAT-WING

Hook: Straight eye, standard length
Tail: Coarse white bucktail, spun around the hook with a longer bunch of
         sparse white bucktail tied on top, over this is a single olive schlappen
         hackle tied flat, curving down, and a few strands of gold Flashabou
         on the side, extending beyond the bucktail
Body: Braided pearl Mylar, wrapped
Collar: Coarse white bucktail, fairly long
Wing: Sparse white bucktail over which is light blue bucktail and pearl
         crystal flash, over which is sparse yellow bucktail, over which is
         sparse olive bucktail, topped with longer peacock herl
Head: White

Bill Peabody of Portsmouth, Rhode Island, developed this pattern after
the flat-wing streamers of Ken Abrames, a well known local fly tier and
angler. This is a great fly for stripers, blues, weakfish and bonito. It can be
modified to imitate a wide range of baitfish.

RICHARDS' BAY ANCHOVY

Hook:	Straight eye, standard length
Tail:	Very fine white streamer hair (Richards uses a 50-50 silk and lamb's wool blend obtained at a fabric store) evenly surrounding the hook shank
Body:	Thread wrapped over the butts of the tail
Throat:	Very fine white streamer hair
Wing:	Very fine white streamer hair over which is golden olive craft fur
Sides:	One strand of pearl Flashabou on each side
Eyes:	Peel-off, stick-on eyes, silver with black pupils
Head:	Epoxy from the eyes forward

This is Carl Richards' accurate rendering of a tiny anchovy that's abundant in most inshore southern waters. The illustrated fly is tied on a size 8 hook; Richards has landed ". . . big snook and 20 pound tarpon on this pattern tied in this size."

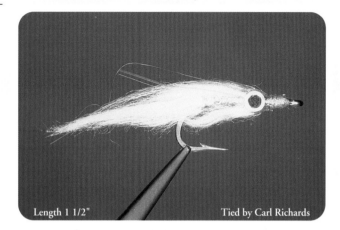

Length 1 1/2" Tied by Carl Richards

RICHARDS' PINFISH

Hook:	Straight eye, standard length
Tail:	V-cut dun hackle secured inside a section of fluorescent green Everglow tubing
Skirt:	Fine white streamer hair (silk and lamb's wool) with gold and pearl Flashabou on the sides
Body:	Fine white streamer hair, tied on the top and bottom in sections along the shank length, colored in alternating bands of light blue. Also color the tips of upper body brown, and make a brown spot at the gill position
Throat:	Colored with a red marking pen
Sides:	Gold and light blue crystal flash
Eyes:	Peel-off, stick-on prismatic eyes
Head:	Epoxy from the eyes forward

Pinfish are abundant along the inshore waters of the southeastern coastal states and provide forage for redfish, snook and tarpon.

Length 4" Tied by Carl Richards

RICHARDS' SCALED SARDINE

Hook:	Straight eye, standard length
Tail:	Fine white streamer hair (silk and lamb's wool)
Body:	Small bunches of fine white streamer hair, secured along the bottom of the hook at equal intervals, tapering up towards the head
Wing:	Pearl crystal flash over which is gold craft fur
Eyes:	Peel-off, stick-on prismatic eyes
Head:	Marked green on top, gold underneath and well coated with epoxy

Sardines are small, or immature, herring and often comprise a considerable part of a fish's diet. Carl Richards' approach to designing his baitfish imitations is consistent with his methodology used when matching natural insects for trout. He is studying the gamefish, learning about their feeding habits, and then matching specific baitfish for each location fished.

Length 2 1/2" Tied by Carl Richards

Length 4"   Tied by Matt Vinciguerra

SALTY BEADY EYE

Hook: Straight eye, standard length
Tail: Four white saddle hackles curving out
Lateral line: Wrap the hook shank with white thread and overwrap with fine monofilament
Bead head: Over a base of thread clamp a hollow brass bead in place and secure with wraps of thread
Throat: Red thread, built up behind the bead
Overbody: Hollow silver Mylar tubing, slipped over the hook eye, half pulled back above and half below, secured at the rear with white thread and unravelled as shown (before securing and unravelling the Mylar, color the upper half with a blue marker)
Eye: Black pupil on the brass bead
Note: Once the body is in place and the pupil has been added, coat eye and body with epoxy.

Originated by Matt Vinciguerra for weakfish (seatrout) and striped bass.

Length 4 1/2"   Tied by Lou Tabory

SAND EEL

Hook: Straight eye, standard or long shank
Wing: White bucktail or similar, over which is pearl crystal flash topped by olive synthetic hair or peacock herl, all dressed very sparsely
Body: White bucktail, over which is pearl crystal flash and olive synthetic hair (which is a continuation from the wing) all wrapped to the bend with strips of clear vinyl and coated with vinyl cement (it is important to keep the materials separated so that the olive top doesn't mix with the white bottom)
Eyes: Painted (optional)
Note: A variation is tied in the same fashion with a black bucktail wing and a black wool body coated with epoxy.

This was Lou Tabory's earliest creation, which he describes as "an ugly fly that catches fish." Sand eels are long, thin and nearly transparent. Imitations must be sparse and sink quickly. A fly with these properties can be fished below heavy concentrations of natural bait, and is more easily seen.

Length 4"   Tied by Jack Gartside

SAND LANCE

Hook: Straight eye, long or standard length
Tail: Pearl or Multi-Light Glimmer or crinkled Mylar
Body: Pearl or Multi-Light Glimmer or crinkled Mylar, wrapped around the hook shank
Wing: Sparse pearl or Multi-Light Glimmer or crinkled Mylar surrounding the hook. With a waterproof marking pen, color the uppermost wing fibers brown
Head: Brown
Eyes: Fluorescent green with black pupils
Note: Using various colors of Glimmer and marking pens, Gartside ties everything from little minnows to needlefish and full-size eels.

Jack Gartside designed this sand eel pattern because it's simple to tie, yet very effective. The entire fly is constructed of only one material and thread.

SCHOOLIE

Hook: Keel hook; two flies tied on a single hook as shown
Underbody: Wrap silver oval or braided tinsel over the area where the epoxy heads will be made, before applying the wings
Wings: Light green over which is light gray Ultra Hair and a single strand of pearl crystal flash as a lateral line
Heads: Epoxy
Eyes: Peel-off, stick-on prismatic eyes with black pupils
Throats: Painted red with a marking pen
Note: After the eyes and mouth have been applied add a final light coat of epoxy over each entire head

Bob Popovics created this unique double (and sometimes triple) baitfish fly to imitate tiny minnows bunched together as part of a larger school. Large predators feeding in schools of small minnows can't pick out singles so they simply open their mouths and go for stray bunches.

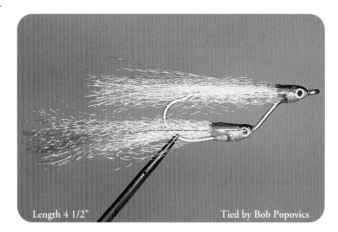
Length 4 1/2" Tied by Bob Popovics

SEA BRAT

Hook: Straight eye, standard length
Wing: Four white hackles curving in, outside of which are a couple of strands of pearl Flashabou on each side
Collar: Two hot pink and two hot red hackles mixed together
Head: A few turns of pink Estaz chenille, in front of which is white pearlescent Estaz chenille, finished off in front with a band of fluorescent red thread followed by white thread

This is a bright and easy-to-tie streamer that can be dressed in a variety of color combinations. Its developer, Oscar Feliu of Lady Lake, Florida, says that the Sea Brats are excellent on redfish, seatrout, mangrove snapper and the occasional snook or ladyfish.

Length 4" Tied by Oscar Feliu

SEA SNAPPER

Hook: Straight eye, long shank
Tail: White FisHair or bucktail
Body: White sparkle yarn, heavy
Rib: Flat silver Mylar tinsel
Throat: White FisHair or bucktail
Wing: Short white FisHair or bucktail over which is longer teal blue FisHair over which is dark blue FisHair or bucktail
Cheeks: Mallard breast or flank, lacquered
Eyes: Painted black with yellow pupils

Bruce Dorn designed this streamer to imitate the "snappers" that are abundant in the late summer and early fall in the bays and tidal creeks off New York and New Jersey. Snappers are what the local surf and jetty fishermen call immature bluefish that are a major source of food for larger fish.

Length 4" Tied by Bruce Dorn

Length 3"   Tied by Dick Stewart

SEA-DUCER, ORANGE & WHITE

Hook: Straight eye, standard length
Wing: Four white saddle hackles, curving out
Collar: White and orange hackle, wrapped dry fly style

Veteran saltwater angler, Chico Fernandez of Miami, popularized this variation of the Rhodes' Tarpon Fly (which see) that's a proven all around saltwater attractor. Lefty Kreh particularly likes this fly in red and white for redfish. The stiff hackle collar helps keep the fly suspended in the water, making this design best for shallow-water fishing.

Length 4"   Tied by George Kesel

SHINEABOU MULLET

Hook: Straight eye, standard length
Tail: White bucktail about twice the length of the hook shank, over which are 8 to 10 fluorescent gray hackles plus sparse silver and gold Flashabou or crystal flash on each side
Underbody: Lead wire wrapped to the middle of the shank
Body: Silver-gray Antron dubbing over the lead wire
Skirt: Silver-gray marabou stripped from the stem, applied as a collar
Throat: Fluff from the base of a red dyed hackle, a bunch on each side
Wing: Peacock herl on top, extending about halfway over the tail
Head and collar: Silver-gray deer body hair, spun and trimmed to shape
Eyes: Solid plastic

This is a saltwater mullet variation of Jimmy Nix's popular freshwater Shineabou baitfish series.

Length 2"   Tied by Jim Grace

SILVER BELLE

Hook: Straight eye, standard length
Tail: Silver Flashabou
Wing: Silver Flashabou, tied in three equally-spaced bunches, ascending in size from the rear to the front
Body: White thread
Head: White
Weedguard: Stainless steel wire

Originated by Glen Puopolo for snook, the Silver Belle is one of Captain Jim Grace's best snook flies. It is usually tied in small sizes.

SILVERSIDES

Hook: Straight eye, standard length or long shank
Tail: White goat hair as long as the shank of the hook
Body: Silver braided Mylar, well lacquered
Wing: Peacock herl over which is white goat hair, both quite sparse
Head: White
Eye: Painted yellow with a black pupil
Note: If you anticipate fishing this fly in rips, or rough surf, Brown suggests using stiffer bucktail in place of the goat hair.

This is an effective imitation of the Atlantic silverside. It was developed in the mid 1960s by Don Brown of Kingston, Massachusetts. Although silversides are very small, they're abundant along the northern portion of the east coast and travel in large schools, providing great forage for striped bass and bluefish. Originally Brown tied this fly for sea-run brown trout, which are known locally as "Salters."

Length 3" Tied by Don Brown

SNOOK FLY

Hook: Straight eye, standard length
Wing: (Tied in at the rear of the hook, above the barb) Natural polar bear hair or similar, over which are a few strands of pearl Flashabou (or crystal flash) and four white hackles
Body: White thread or floss, to about the middle of the shank
Collar: Natural polar bear hair or similar
Topping: Several strands of peacock herl
Head: White thread or floss
Weedguard: Stainless wire, size #5

Developed by Jim Grace of Naples, Florida, for casting directly into thick mangrove roots. This fly resembles a Lefty's Deceiver tied toward the back of the hook. It has also been called a Mangrove Snook Fly.

Length 3 1/2" Tied by Jim Grace

SOFT HACKLE STREAMER

Hook: Straight eye, standard length
Underwing: About four strands of pearl Flashabou
Wing: Fluorescent green marabou, folded, tied in by the tip slightly behind the eye of the hook and wrapped
Collar: Mallard flank, natural or dyed
Head: Fluorescent green
Eye: Yellow with black pupil

This is one of Jack Gartside's favorite baitfish imitations that's been effective on most species of saltwater fish. The size of the fly is limited by the length of marabou plume fibers; it's most effective in small sizes, imitating smaller baitfish. The Magic Minnow, a similar Gartside pattern, is even smaller and consists of a little Flashabou and a collar of mallard flank.

Length 3" Tied by Jack Gartside

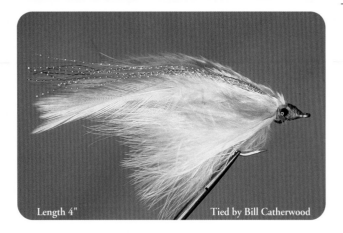

Length 4" Tied by Bill Catherwood

SPRAT

Hook:	Straight eye, standard length
Underwing:	A single white, pearl gray, light pink and light blue marabou feather, attached in this order
Wing:	On each side a set of two light blue hackles outside of which are two pearl gray hackles
Sides:	Pink, light blue and dark blue crystal flash
Eyes:	Solid glass
Head:	Blue

Baby herring (or Sprat) are a favorite of striped bass, mackerel and tuna, and are found both offshore and inshore.

Length 4" Tied by Jim Stewart

STEWART'S D-3 BAITFISH

Hook:	Straight eye, standard length
Wing:	Four white hackles curving in, over which is silver Flashabou and silver crystal flash, mixed
Skirt:	Gray marabou
Butt:	Fluorescent pink chenille
Collar:	White deer body hair over the upper part of the fly
Head:	Spun white deer body hair, trimmed as shown and cemented on the bottom and front ⅓
Eyes:	Solid plastic

This is a great diving minnow or wounded baitfish imitation that has recently had a lot of success. Jim Stewart said that it has been especially deadly on king mackerel.

Length 3 1/2" Tied by Jim Stewart

STEWART'S DARK INVADER

Hook:	Straight eye, standard length
Wing:	Four black marabou plumes tied face to face outside of which on each side is a webby purple hackle and several strands of blue Flashabou, over the top is silver crystal flash
Throat:	Light gray marabou
Eyes:	Solid brown plastic with black pupils
Head:	Black with a narrow band of orange in front of the eyes

This is a dark, evil-looking streamer that was developed by Jim Stewart and will take everything from snook and tarpon, to striped bass and bluefish. It works well in low light conditions.

STEWART'S LUCKY WIGGLER RUNT

Hook: Straight eye, long shank or standard length
Tail: Deep pink bucktail over which are four broad cerise hackles on the inside and two hot orange grizzly hackles on the outside, with a mixture of copper Flashabou and copper crystal flash on top
Butt: Fluorescent rose chenille
Collar: Orange deer body hair on the sides and cerise on top
Head: Orange, cerise, pale yellow and pink deer body hair stacked over pink deer body hair, trimmed as shown and cemented in front and on the bottom
Eyes: Solid plastic

"This floating, popping, diving fly is a real redfish killer on the flats," says Jim Stewart, who ties it in many colors including yellow, black, chartreuse and red and white. In various colors and sizes cobia, seatrout and snook will also bite Stewart's Lucky Wigglers.

Length 3 1/2"   Tied by Jim Stewart

STEWART'S SNOOK-A-ROO, MIDNIGHT

Hook: Straight eye, standard length
Tail: Dyed brown bucktail over which are three pairs of dark furnace hackles curving out, over which is copper Flashabou and black crystal flash
Butt: Fluorescent orange chenille
Skirt: Red marabou on each side to imitate gills
Collar: Black deer body hair on each side and brown on top
Head: Brown and black deer body hair stacked over black, trimmed as shown and cemented in front and on the bottom
Eyes: Solid plastic

Jim Stewart of Tampa, was the recipient of the Federation of Fly Fishers 1992 Southeastern Council Fly Tier of the Year award. His versatile floating-diving Snook-A-Roo is dressed in many colors for a variety of inshore gamefish. This one works best at night, in shallow water.

Length 4"   Tied by Jim Stewart

STICK CANDY

Hook: Straight eye, long shank
Underbody: Silver Mylar tinsel
Wing: White, over which is gray Ultra Hair with sparse silver Mylar on each side, secured at the eye with white thread which is colored with a marking pen
Body: Epoxy over the forward portion of the wing and underbody
Eyes: Peel-off, stick-on silver prismatic eyes with black pupils
Gills and mouth: Painted on with a red marking pen
Note: After the eyes and mouth have been applied add a final light coat of epoxy over the entire body.

This is part of the Pop-Fleye series that was developed by Bob Popovics of Seaside Park, New Jersey, for fly fishing in the surf. Stick Candy may be distinguished from Surf Candy flies (which see) by the longer shank hook which helps in imitating long, skinny baitfish like sand eels.

Length 5"   Tied by Bob Popovics

Atlantic & Gulf Coast Baitfish

Length 4" Tied by Bob Popovics

SURF CANDY

Hook: Straight eye, standard length
Extended tail: Badger hackle (trimmed as shown) epoxied to one end of a piece of 30 lb. monofilament, which is then sheathed with silver braided Mylar, cemented so it won't unravel, and set aside
Underbody: Braided pearlescent Mylar tubing, wrapped
Wing: Polar Bear Ultra Hair over which is the "extended tail" section, over which is Polar Bear Ultra Hair and gray Ultra Hair. Tie in at the head with white thread and color on top
Body and head: Front portion of the wing and underbody, saturated with epoxy
Eyes: Peel-off, stick-on prismatic eyes with black pupils
Gills: Painted red with a marking pen
Note: Add a final light coat of epoxy over the entire body.

This is another of Bob Popovic's realistic Pop-Fleyes that can be tied to imitate a variety of baitfish. Pop-Fleyes cast and sink well, and never foul.

Length 6" Tied by John Bottko

SURFIN' WOOLY

Hook: Straight eye, long shank
Tail: White bucktail flanked by six long white saddle hackles, curving in, outside of which are strands of pearl crystal flash
Underbody: Lead wire
Body: Thick white chenille
Hackle: White, soft and webby, palmered over the body
Eyes: Hollow or solid plastic, yellow with black pupils

John Bottko of Jacksonville, Florida, says that "Redfish will cruise right on the edge of the surf looking for bait that is being moved back and forth in the breakers." The Surfin' Wooly gets down deep where these cruising reds feed. It should also work on almost any species that chases its food in the surf.

Length 7" Tied by Lou Tabory

TABORY'S SLAB SIDE

Hook: Straight eye, standard length
Wing: White bucktail over which is tan synthetic hair and pearl Flashabou, over which is deep rose bucktail over which is gray bucktail topped by peacock herl
Eyes: Glass or lead eyes, yellow with black pupils
Collar: White deer body hair
Head: Spun white deer body hair, trimmed flat on the sides as shown
Note: This fly may be tied with either a bucktail or marabou wing using the colors that match the baitfish you want to imitate. The flat slab side shape of the trimmed deer hair head and collar is critical to the performance of this fly.

Lou Tabory, author of *Inshore Fly Fishing*, says that the Slab Side was tied to imitate the flat shape of a herring or bunker (menhaden), both of which are major forage for east coast striped bass and bluefish. "What I got," says Tabory, "was a fly that fluttered like a crippled baitfish."

TABORY'S SNAKE FLY

Hook: Straight eye, standard length or long shank
Tail: Yellow ostrich plumes or very narrow saddle hackle, over which is yellow crystal flash
Body: Yellow tying thread
Wing: Two plumes of yellow marabou
Collar: Yellow or fluorescent yellow deer body hair
Head: Yellow or fluorescent yellow deer body hair, spun and trimmed to a small and compact head shape that is slightly rounded on top and flat on the bottom

Tabory credits Eric Leiser's Angus (which see) for inspiring the development of the Snake Fly, which he considers his "most useful (saltwater) pattern." The clipped deer-hair head of the Snake Fly creates a turbulence which causes the the tail and wing to wiggle seductively. Fished with an intermediate flyline, the fly will dive below the surface and ". . . wiggle towards the surface."

Length 5"   Tied by Lou Tabory

TABORY'S SURFBOARD FOAM FLY

Hook: Straight eye, long shank
Tail: Rose pink bucktail over white bucktail, or pink and white saddle hackles
Body: Shaped from a piece of "surfboard foam," slit lengthwise and cemented to the hook shank, secured with thread, coated with epoxy and painted
Eyes: Painted yellow with black pupils
Note: After the eyes have been painted, coat the entire body with a thin coat of epoxy. It should be tied in any shape or color that's consistent with the minnows in your area.

Lou Tabory designed the Surfboard Foam Fly "to work like a floating minnow type spinning lure." He further suggests that it should be fished to ". . . dip below the surface then float to the top," imitating an injured baitfish helplessly struggling to swim away. The unique properties of surfboard foam make this fly a great floater.

Length 7"   Tied by Lou Tabory

TOM'S BLUE BACK HERRING

Hook: Straight eye, standard length
Wing: White bucktail, tied short, over which is (in this order) pearl crystal flash, Polar Bear Ultra Hair, pearl crystal flash, Polar Bear Ultra Hair, purple crystal flash, pearl Flashabou, mixed blue and green Flashabou, blue, green and olive Ultra Hair
Gills: Red hackle barbs
Head and collar: Natural lamb's wool, spun and trimmed to shape and colored with marking pens as shown
Eyes: Glass, yellow with black pupils

Tom Piccolo of the Sportsman's Den tells us that herring enter Long Island Sound in late spring, continue northward, and re-appear in late fall. When they are present, bass and blues feed on them heavily. In the spring Piccolo ties this fly about 4" long, but when the herring return in late October he prefers a fly that measures 6" or 7" long. Either way, you'll want a 10 weight line or better to throw this fly.

Length 7"   Tied by Tom Piccolo

Length 8"   Tied by Tom Piccolo

TOM'S BUNKER FLY

Hook: Straight eye, standard length
Wing: White bucktail over which is (in this order) sparse white FisHair, pearl crystal flash, white FisHair, rainbow crystal flash, white Ultra Hair, rainbow crystal flash, fluorescent pink Ultra Hair and crystal flash, pale yellow Ultra Hair, root beer crystal flash, tan Ultra Hair, olive crystal flash, olive Ultra Hair and peacock crystal flash
Gills: Red marabou
Head and collar: Natural lamb's wool, spun trimmed to shape and colored with marking pens as shown
Eyes: Glass, glued in place

The largest striped bass and bluefish caught in Long Island Sound seem to be taken along the Connecticut shore. From July until the fish head south in late October, large "bunker" (mossbunker or menhaden) are a primary forage and Tom Piccolo's Bunker pattern is one of his best.

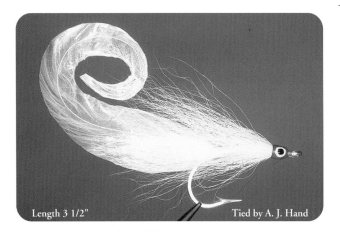

Length 3 1/2"   Tied by A. J. Hand

TWISTED SISTER

Hook: Straight eye, standard length
Tail: Prepare a tail by taking one white hackle, surround it with very sparse bucktail, saturate both with clear silicone rubber and flatten into a spiral on wax paper. Once dry (about 2 hours) peel off, trim away any excess silicone, and tie it to the hook
Body: Flat pearl or silver Mylar tinsel
Collar: White bucktail
Head: Red
Eyes: Painted yellow with a black pupil
Note: Tied in many colors on a size 2/0 hook or larger. The heavy hook balances the fly and produces the best action.

The Twisted Sister was developed by A.J. Hand who describes it as being something "like a Lefty's Deceiver (which see) with a wiggling action." It works best fished in a current or with steady retrieve.

Length 5"   Tied by Debie Waterman

WATERMAN'S SILVER OUTCAST

Hook: Straight eye, standard length
Body: Flat silver Mylar tinsel
Wing: White bucktail over which is yellow bucktail and turquoise blue bucktail, topped by peacock herl over which is pearl Flashabou
Cheeks: Jungle cock (optional)
Head: Fluorescent red

Noted author and outdoor writer Charles Waterman says that the Silver Outcast "started as an elongated Silver Doctor with some materials missing . . . given to him on an Everglades creek." On that day it was far and away the top producer for snook and small tarpon. The fly that evolved ". . . for 30 years, has been the most consistent thing we've used in saltwater . . . not spectacular, just regularly productive."

WHITE WATER WITCH

Hook: Straight eye, standard or long shank
Tail: Black bucktail or FisHair
Body: Silver braided Mylar, wrapped
Wing: Black bucktail or FisHair extending about half the length of the
          tail
Throat: Red bucktail
Head: Black

Ray Smith is a saltwater fly-fishing pioneer from Newport, Rhode Island, who developed the White Water Witch for fishing in heavy surf. Lou Tabory suggests tying it about 6" long and fishing it "in the rolling surf, along a cliff."

Length 4 1/2"   Tied by Jamie Dickinson

WHITLOCK'S EEL WORM

Hook: Straight eye, standard length
Wing: Four to six long and narrow light ginger variant saddle hackles,
          outside of which are two short light ginger variant spade or hen
          hackles, over which is sparse pearl crystal flash
Eyes: Silver bead chain or chromed lead dumbbell eyes tied on the
          underside of the hook
Hackle: Soft light ginger variant, wrapped behind and in front of the eyes
Head: Fluorescent red
Note: May be tied effectively in a wide range of colors.

Dave Whitlock developed the Eel Worm in the mid 1970s for largemouth and smallmouth bass. It has proven itself to be a tremendously effective design that works in saltwater as well.

Length 5"   Tied by Farrow Allen

WOLF'S ANCHOVIE

Hook: Straight eye, long shank
Tail: White or chartreuse marabou and silver crystal flash
Underbody: Silver, or silver and pearl crystal flash twisted together,
          wrapped up the hook shank with several extra wraps behind the
          hook eye to build up the head. On the underside secure a piece
          of 20 lb. monofilament at the head and tail, forming a frame for
          the body
Body: Epoxy shaped as shown, with a little pearl glitter mixed into the
          epoxy
Eyes: Peel-off, stick-on eyes, white with black pupils, epoxy coated
Gills: Red lacquer

Dick Wolf, of New York's Salty Flyrodders, developed this pattern for bonito and small tuna in waters around Long Island and Connecticut. During the early fall these fish feed heavily on anchovies. Wolf ties the fly on long stainless-steel hooks to ". . . survive bluefish strikes and hook-ups without using wire or heavy monofilament for the leader-shy bonito."

Length 3"   Tied by Dick Wolf

Length 1" Tied by Tony Route

ALEVIN

Hook: Straight eye, long shank, usually sizes 6 to 10
Underbody: Lead wire, covered with white thread (optional)
Body: Pearl braided Mylar
Tail: Pearl braided Mylar from the body, unravelled
Throat (egg sac): Bright orange marabou, clipped short
Eyes: Small silver bead chain, secured with white thread

Tony Route of Anchorage, Alaska, originally designed the Alevin for fishing in freshwater, ". . . but during the summer of 1983 I used it in Alaska's saltwater with great success . . . for sea run cutthroat and Dolly Varden." An alevin is a juvenile chum or pink salmon that migrates to sea before absorbing its yolk sac. They usually migrate in great numbers and cause quite a feeding frenzy in the estuaries and river mouths.

Length 8" Tied by Dan Blanton

BLANTON'S BAY-DELTA EELET

Hook: Straight eye, standard length
Wing #1:   Black FisHair outside of which are half a dozen long black hackles with sparse black crystal flash on each side
Body: Black chenille to about the middle of the hook shank
Wing #2:   Six more black hackles and a single grizzly hackle on each side, topped with black crystal flash
Eyes: Silver bead chain
Head: Black chenille built up around the bead-chain eyes
Note: Usually tied on about a size 4/0 hook.

Originated in 1969 on the Pacific Coast for striped bass fishing by Dan Blanton of San Jose, California. By tying the wing in two parts, the forward section (Wing # 2) cocks up and "humps" over the chenille giving the appearence of bulk. Blanton says the Bay-Delta Eelet is definitely "a big fish fly."

Length 3 1/2" Tied by Dan Blanton

BLANTON'S DEEPWATER WHISTLER,
YELLOW-RED

Hook: Straight eye, standard length
Tail: Yellow bucktail and two yellow hackles curving out
Wing #1:   Advance the (red) tying thread about halfway up the hook shank and tie in two more yellow hackles curving out
Wing #2:   Advance thread up to the normal wing position and attach 2 yellow hackles and a grizzly hackle on each side, curving out. Over this add silver Flashabou and peacock herl
Throat: Yellow bucktail as long as the wing
Collar: Red marabou
Eyes: Silver bead chain secured in front of the throat with red thread

Dan Blanton introduced the Deepwater Whistlers in 1973 for San Francisco Bay stripers. Later he found them to be very effective for tarpon and snook in Costa Rica.

BLANTON'S FATAL ATTRACTION

Hook: Straight eye, standard length
Tail: Silver Flashabou
Body: Pearl braided Mylar (take a turn of the Mylar underneath and to the rear of the Flashabou tail)
Throat: White hackle wound as a collar
Wing: Sparse white bucktail over which is sparse blue bucktail and pearl crystal flash, with peacock herl over all
Eyes: Silver bead chain
Head: White

Dan Blanton calls this a good "general saltwater pattern" that has shown itself to be notably effective for bonito and small tuna.

Length 2"   Tied by Dan Blanton

BLANTON'S LIME PUNCH

Hook: Straight eye, standard length
Tail: Fluorescent lime green bucktail over which is kelly green Flashabou
Body: Chartreuse crystal flash
Throat: Fluorescent green hackle applied as a collar
Wing: Chartreuse crystal flash, fluorescent green-dyed grizzly hackle on each side and peacock over all (don't trim the herl butts, later they will be pulled forward over the top of the chenille head)
Eyes: Silver bead chain
Head: Fluorescent green chenille with peacock herl pulled forward over the top and secured with fluorescent green thread

Dan Blanton developed the Punch series in 1971. Using the same design, the Sábalo Punch is silver and grizzly with an orange collar and fluorescent red head. Sábalo is the Spanish word for tarpon. The Tropical Punch is gold, yellow and orange-grizzly, a yellow collar and fluorescent red head.

Length 3 1/2"   Tied by Dan Blanton

BLANTON'S SAR-MUL-MAC ,
BLUE MACKEREL

Hook: Straight eye, standard length
Throat: White bucktail, long
Wing: About ten white hackles, over which is sparse blue bucktail over which is chartreuse crystal flash and peacock herl over the top (don't trim the herl butts, later they will be pulled forward over the top of the chenille head). On each side is a single well-marked grizzly hackle dyed blue, and silver Flashabou
Eyes: Glass taxidermy, or similar
Head: A band of red chenille (indicating a throat) followed by white chenille, built up around the eyes, and peacock herl over the top

Blanton developed the Sar-mul-mac style in the early 1970s as a saltwater baitfish imitation which, when tied in different colors, represents various species including sardines (SAR), mullet (MUL) and mackerel (MAC).

Length 6"   Tied by Dan Blanton

Length 5 1/2"   Tied by Dan Blanton

BLANTON'S CHARTREUSE
FLASHTAIL WHISTLER

Hook: Straight eye, standard length
Wing: Fluorescent green bucktail, a long bunch of kelly green Flashabou and another bunch of fluorescent green bucktail. On each side add a little chartreuse crystal flash and a single grizzly hackle dyed fluorescent green
Body: About two turns of fluorescent green chenille in front of the wing
Collar: Webby fluorescent green hackle, tied full
Eyes: Silver bead chain, attached with fluorescent green tying thread

The Flashtail Whistler is a Whistler variation that's been enhanced with Flashabou and crystal flash.

Length 4"   Tied by Dan Blanton

BLANTON'S WHITE WHISTLER

Hook: Straight eye, standard length
Wing: White bucktail tied full, outside of which is a narrow strip of red bucktail
Body: Large red chenille, about two turns directly in front of the wing
Collar: Webby white hackle, tied full
Eyes: Silver bead chain, attached with red tying thread

This is another variation of the Whistler that uses no hackles in the wing, but maintains the basic Whistler shape and shares the short red chenille body, soft hackle collar and bead chain eyes. The common element that gave the Whistlers their name is the bead-chain eyes that "whistle" while being cast.

Length 4 1/2"   Tied by Dan Blanton

BLANTON'S WHITE WHISTLER,
RED/GRIZZLY

Hook: Straight eye, standard length
Wing: White bucktail, tied full and two grizzly hackles per side curving out, one up and the other down as shown
Body: Two turns of red chenille directly in front of the wing
Collar: Webby red hackle, tied full
Eyes: Silver bead chain, secured with red thread in front of the collar

This is one of Dan Blanton's early Whistlers from a series that he introduced in 1964. Like many of Blanton's flies, the Whistler is more of a style of fly than a specific fly; a general order of basic components from which to build. Two other popular Blanton originals tied in this way include one with yellow bucktail and grizzly wing and red collar, and black bucktail and grizzly wing and red collar.

BUNNY BLENNY, BLACK

Hook: Rubber worm hook with wire weedguard, that can be found in shops that carry freshwater bass gear; the weedguard should be moved out of the way while you tie the fly
Tail: Black rabbit fur strip, skin side down
Body: Black cross-cut rabbit fur strip, wrapped up the shank
Eyes: Chrome lead dumbbell eyes
Head: Blue
Note: Also tied in white, yellow and olive.

A blenny is an eel-like fish that's common in the bays along the rocky coastline of Oregon and Washington. Both rockfish and ling are very fond of blennies and this pattern gets down deep where they feed. John Shewey acknowledges that the steel weedguard keeps the fly basically weed free "... but also serves a more important function in preventing the long rabbit-fur strip tail from wrapping around the hook."

Length 6"   Tied by John Shewey

CHARTREUSE EVERGLOW FLY

Hook: Straight eye, standard length
Underbody: Lead wire (optional) and white yarn, chenille or floss to cover the lead or build a base for the body
Body: Fluorescent green Everglow tubing, secured with white thread
Tail: Unravelled Everglow tubing from the body
Throat: Fluorescent green hackle applied as a collar
Wing: White calftail over which are strips of unravelled fluorescent green Everglow

Tony Route introduced this fly to Alaska's Prince William Sound, shortly after Everglow appeared on the market in about 1984. Since then he has fished it with success "... for silver and king salmon wherever they can be approached in saltwater in Alaska."

Length 1 1/2"   Tied by Tony Route

FENDER FLY, LIME NYLON

Hook: Straight eye, standard length
Wing: Three doubled bunches of polar bear Ultra Hair over which is silver crystal flash, doubled yellow Ultra Hair and green Ultra Hair (each doubled bunch of hair is tied along the shank in front of and over the preceding bunch)
Fender face: Prismatic Mylar sheet, reinforced on the back with strapping tape, cut to shape, folded around the front part of the wing
Eyes: "Sew-on Snaps." The snaps are connected through a hole made in the fender face with a needle. They are snapped together and secured by tapping with a hammer on a flat surface. The eye and pupil are made by placing colored epoxy in the cupped surface

Rob Ransom designed this fly after Dave Whitlock's Prismatic Minnow and a Japanese lure made with dried fish skins "... folded over hook shanks to make small baitfish imitations." Variations feature wings of bucktail, marabou or any other suitable materials in your choice of colors.

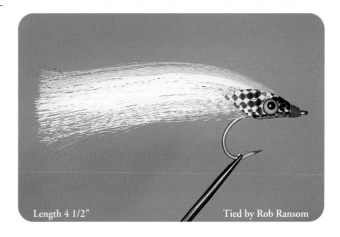
Length 4 1/2"   Tied by Rob Ransom

Length 1 1/2"   Tied by Tony Route

FLASH FLY

Hook: Straight eye, standard length
Underbody: Lead wire (optional)
Tail: Silver Flashabou
Body: Silver braided poly flash
Collar: Red hackle
Wing: Sparse red calftail or bucktail over which is silver Flashabou
Head: Red

Tony Route of Anchorage, Alaska, author of *Flyfishing Alaska* and *Flies for Alaska* sent us the Flash Fly. He says it likely developed on Kodiak Island around the Karluk River estuary where silver salmon are frequently caught in saltwater on flies. In estuaries throughout Alaska, it has been good for sea-run Dolly Varden and king salmon.

Length 3"   Tied by Joe Butorac

FLASHY LADY

Hook: Straight eye, long shank
Wing: Pink bucktail, tied 360 degrees around the hook like a collar
Head and collar: Unravelled pearl braided Mylar tied Thunder Creek or bullethead style, secured with transparent thread
Eyes: Black paint, epoxy over
Note: Two popular variations are tied with blue or green bucktail

Designed by longtime commercial fly tier Joe Butorac of Arlington, Washington, for casting to schools of Pacific salmon in the bays and estuaries of the Pacific Northwest. In a variety of colors, the Flashy Lady has been deadly on small coho salmon up to 5 lbs. and a variety of other saltwater fish as well.

Length 4"   Tied by Steve Probasco

FROGGY'S TANDEM HERRING

Hooks: Straight eyes, standard length connected with 50 lb. monofilament. The trailing hook should be close enough to touch the front hook and the point should face up
Body: Silver braided Mylar or similar (on both hooks)
Wing: White FisHair over which is pearl and bronze Flashabou with peacock herl over all
Head: White
Eye: Black paint

Steve Probasco is a Washington state fly tier who developed the Froggy Tandem Herring for Pacific salmon, more specifically chinook and coho. He calls it "my version of the perfect baitfish," and indeed it has brought many salmon to the boat.

JANSSEN HALFBEAK

Hook: Down eye, long shank
Wing: White bucktail, flared around the ball of chenille over which are four black hackles tied in on top and curving in. Next add three white hackles on each side curving out and a single longer grizzly hackle on each side curving in. Spread over the top are six to eight brownish olive hackles tied flat and curving down
Collar: Several wraps of olive marabou in front of which is a bunch of golden olive marabou on each side and several more wraps of olive in front, all pulled back and tied down
Head: Brownish olive with a golden olive as shown, covered with epoxy
Eyes: Solid glass

Hal Janssen developed this fly around 1959 for San Francisco Bay striped bass.

Length 6"   Tied by Farrow Allen

KRYSTAL FLASH CANDLEFISH

Hook: Straight eye, standard length
Wing: Tied Thunder Creek style: fine Polar White FisHair on the bottom, surrounded by pearl Krystal Flash and topped by olive Krystal Flash over which is peacock Krystal Flash, secured with transparent sewing thread
Eyes: Painted yellow with black pupils, coat eyes and head with epoxy
Note: A monofilament loop tied on top of the hook, extending rearward beyond the bend, maintains color separation and helps keep the wing from fouling.

The candlefish is a Pacifc Northwest smelt that represents a very important inshore forage for Pacific salmon in saltwater bays and estuaries. Joe Butorac's imitation is effective and versatile.

Length 5"   Tied by Joe Butorac

LAMBUTH CANDLEFISH

Hook: Straight eye, standard length or long shank
Body: Flat silver tinsel
Wing: Mixture of pale blue and pale green polar bear or substitute over which is narrow red polar bear, topped by a mix of French (grayish) blue and a little green polar bear or substitute
Note: Since polar bear is no longer available, dyed bucktail, FisHair or the crystal hair is often substituted

Salmon and sea-run cutthroat feed heavily on candlefish when they are schooling up in estuaries prior to entering fresh water to spawn. Over half a century after its creation, Lechter Lambuth's original design is still one of the best.

Length 3"   Tied by Farrow Allen

Length 5" Tied by Thunder Dragon Flies

PETE'S PERSUADER

Hook: Straight eye, standard length
Wing: Six to ten white hackles outside of which are two grizzly hackles
         and a few strands of pearl crystal flash on each side, over this is
         peacock herl and several more strands of pearl crystal flash
Throat: White rabbit fur and guardhairs
Collar: Natural cream lamb's wool, over the top part of the body only
Head: Natural cream lamb's wool, spun and trimmed as shown
Eyes: Solid plastic

This is a saltwater streamer that was designed by Bob Johns, who is well
known for his similar fly named the Widowmaker.

Length 5" Tied by Nick Curcione

SARDINA

Hook: Straight eye, standard length
Wing: Alternating light blue and very dark brown or black hackles,
         about eight altogether
Collar: A short bunch of white FisHair surrounding the hook shank
Sides: Pearl Flashabou
Eyes: Hollow plastic, yellow
Head: Yellow thread coated with epoxy

Nick Curcione developed this streamer for fishing offshore for big-eye and
yellowfin tuna, skipjack, dorado and the occasional Pacific barracuda.
Sardina is a local Mexican name for a baitfish common in Baja California,
that looks like a cross between a herring and an anchovy.

Length 3" Tied by John Shewey

SHEWEY'S POLAR BEAR CANDLEFISH

Hook: Straight eye, standard length
Wing: White over which is yellow polar bear hair or substitute, pearl
         Flashabou followed by bright green and blue polar bear hair or
         substitute
Eyes: Hollow plastic
Head: Blue
Note: Coat both the head and the eyes with epoxy.

This is part of a series of baitfish imitations designed by John Shewey of
Aumsville, Oregon. Shewey, who is best known for his original steelhead
flies, also ties a herring (see next page) and an anchovy variation. Although
first used for fishing in the surf along Oregon's rocky coastline, Shewey
says "like any good baitfish imitation, these (flies) are effective anywhere
that gamefish feed on small bait."

SHEWEY'S POLAR BEAR HERRING

Hook: Straight eye, standard length
Wing: White Ultra Hair over which is Polar Bear Ultra Hair over which is chartreuse polar bear or substitute, over which is silver Flashabou topped with blue polar bear or substitute
Eyes: Hollow plastic, yellow with black pupils
Head: Blue
Note: Coat both the head and the eyes with epoxy.

Shewey suggests using FisHair as a good substitute for polar bear hair, even though it doesn't have quite as much sheen as the natural hair.

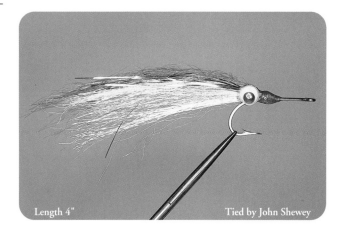

Length 4"   Tied by John Shewey

STREAKER

Hook: Straight eye, standard length
Tail: A small bunch of crinkly white bucktail (optional)
Wing: Several strands of silver or gold Flashabou over which are two narrow grizzly saddle hackles and a small bunch of peacock herl, over which is a matched pair of peacock sword feathers
Collar: Yellow bucktail
Head: Red
Eyes: Painted white with black pupils

Ned Grey designed the Streaker. Its name results from the fact that it seemed to work best when it was retrieved as fast as possible. Soon after tying it, the fly was tested on a trip to Baja where it caught a Roosterfish in excess of 50 pounds. Colors and components may vary, but the peacock sword topping distinguishes this style.

Length 4"   Tied by Jamie Dickinson

WIDOWMAKER

Hook: Straight eye, long shank
Wing: Cerise rabbit fur strip
Body: Cerise fur, applied with a dubbing loop
Throat: Black rabbit fur, divided underneath to appear like two black pectoral fins
Collar: Black lamb's wool, spread evenly over the top half of the fly
Head: Cerise lamb's wool spun and trimmed to shape as shown
Eyes: Solid plastic

The Widowmaker was developed by Bob Johns for large, western brown trout. It has since proven to be effective in a variety of sizes and colors for many saltwater fish as well.

Length 3"   Tied by Thunder Dragon Flies

Length 6" Tied by Steve Abel

Length 11" Tied by Nick Curcione

Length 12" Tied by Jack Samson

ABEL'S ANCHOVY

Hook: Straight eye, standard length
Body: Pearl or silver diamond braid
Wing: Using bucktail or synthetic hair, tie in a large bunch of white hair over which are smaller bunches of green then blue, topped by silver Flashabou, pearl crystal flash and peacock herl
Throat: White bucktail over which is a short bunch of red or orange crystal flash
Head: Clear coat of hot glue over fluorescent yellow thread, with hollow plastic eyes set into the glue

This fly was introduced in 1988 by Steve Abel who is well known for producing quality fly reels. Initially, Abel designed the Anchovy for shark fishing, but says that it has since been an effective fly for tarpon, trevally, bonito, bluefish and dolphin.

BIG-GAME FLY

Front hook: Straight eye, std. length (6/0 to 8/0)
Rear hook: Up eye, reversed bend
Note: The rear hook is at a 45 degree angle to the front hook and connected by a loop of double crimped 90 lb. Sevenstrand wire that is run through the eye and pulled over the hook.
Wing: Bunches of white FishHair, over and outside of which are long white hackles with pearlescent blue Flashabou on top and pearl on the side
Throat: Pearl Flashabou
Head: Blue thread over pearlescent Flashabou covered with epoxy
Eyes: Solid plastic

Nick Curcione developed this offset tandem hook arrangement to help in hooking large offshore billfish, tuna, dorado and sharks.

BILLFISH MULLET, BLUE

Hook: Straight eye, standard length, connected by crimped steel wire leader
Rear wing: White hackles over which are grizzly and light blue hackles splaying out with 2 black hackles, pearl and blue Flashabou and peacock herl over
Body: Pearl braided Mylar over the wire
Throat: White hackles curving down and out
Front wing: Grizzly hackles over which are blue and black hackles all splaying outward, pearl and blue Flashabou and peacock herl over all
Cheeks: Red golden pheasant body feather over which is a white body feather
Eyes: Hollow plastic
Head: Pearl Mylar tubing and red thread

Jack Samson says that sailfish and marlin will eat a balao or mullet streamer nearly every time.

Length 9"   Tied by Bob Popovics

Length 7"   Tied by Bob Popovics

Length 9" overall   Tied by Joe Butorac

BOB'S BIG BOY	BOB'S SQUID BANGER	BUTORAC'S SAILFISH SPECIAL

BOB'S BIG BOY

Hook: Straight eye, standard length
Wing: White Hair-a-bou outside of which is pearlescent rainbow crystal flash
Head: Red lamb's wool evenly distributed all around the wing
Eyes: Peel-off, stick-on prismatic eyes or hollow plastic eyes
Head: Fluorescent red
Note: When the head is finished, comb the wool and Hair-a-bou out and back to provide a fuller, more evenly balanced, streamer

Bob's Big Boys are Popovics' answer to the ideal offshore or big fish fly; they look enormous in the water and almost cast well. This example he calls Cotton Candy. Some of the offshore versions, including one called Mr. Big, are well over a foot long.

BOB'S SQUID BANGER

Hooks: Two straight eye, standard length hooks, each sheathed with white bucktail, tied in tandem and connected with heavy monofilament
Tentacles: Eight yellow schlappen or webby saddle hackles, speckled with a marking pen, and epoxied into eight small holes made around the perimeter of the end of the popper head
Popper head: Dense yellow Livebody foam covered with brown and red spots; drilled through the center for the shock tippet to connect to the tandem hook setup
Eyes: Peel-off, stick-on prismatic eyes

This is an offshore variation of Bob's Banger. When fishing, jam the eye of the front hook into the hole at the rear of the foam popper.

BUTORAC'S SAILFISH SPECIAL

Hooks: 5/0 front hook, 4/0 trailing hook (point up) snelled with 100 lb. monofilament
Tail: White bucktail on the trailing hook
Lower wing: Sixteen white hackles (8 tied vertically over which 8 horizontally)
Sides: Unravelled pearl braided Mylar
Upper wing: 7 blue hackles tied flat
Head: White with blue on top
Eyes: Yellow with black pupils
Popper head: White closed cell foam with solid plastic eyes and a ⅛" diameter plastic tube run lengthwise through the center

The popper head is slipped on to the shock tippet and held in place from 1" to 12" ahead of the fly by a nail knot tied onto the shock tippet. Jim Watt set the 8 lb. IGFA record in 1989 using this pattern.

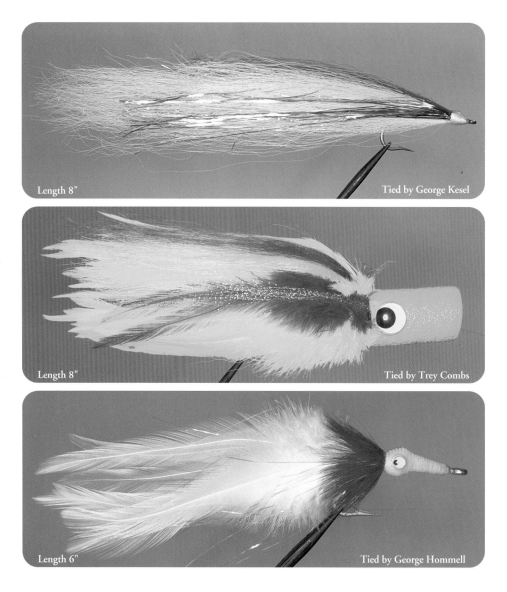

Length 8"   Tied by George Kesel

Length 8"   Tied by Trey Combs

Length 6"   Tied by George Hommell

FERNANDEZ'S BIG FISH FLY

Hook: Straight eye, standard length
Wing: White FisHair tied 360 degrees around the hook shank and very long, over which is a bunch of green followed by blue FisHair, tied shorter, with silver Flashabou on each side, the length of the white FisHair
Head: White

This fly was designed by Chico Fernandez. It can be fished for most species of large offshore gamefish.

GREEN MACHINE

Hooks: Short shank, tied in tandem
Tube: Shock tippet goes through a combination of plastic tubing: inner ⅛" OD tubing extends through the popper head; over this at rear a shorter ¼" OD tube accepts front hook eye; over this is a ⅜" OD tube around which wing is tied
Wing: White bucktail and pearl Flashabou over which fluorescent green bucktail, chartreuse crystal flash and fluorescent green and blue, FisHair. Surrounding this 20 to 30 fluorescent green hackles and 2 blue hackles per side, outside of which is chartreuse and blue crystal flash
Popper head: Fluorescent green; plastic eyes

Combs, the leading authority on steelhead fishing, is also an accomplished billfish angler.

HOMMELL'S EVIL EYE BILLFISH

Hook: Straight eye, standard length
Wing: A small short bunch of white bucktail (optional) and eight white hackles, four on each side curving out, outside of which are strands of pearl Flashabou
Collar: Red hackle
Head: White thread, built up as shown and well cemented or epoxied
Eyes: Small hollow plastic

This is a basic offshore fly that was designed for sailfish by George Hommell of the World Wide Sportsman in Islamorada, Florida. Hommell says that a snelled trailer hook is often added in the construction of this pattern, which can help you get a solid hookup on a large billfish. It's also popular using all pink materials.

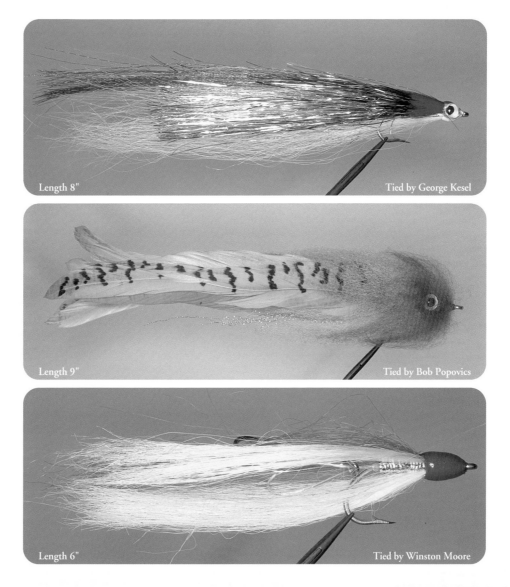

Length 8"   Tied by George Kesel

Length 9"   Tied by Bob Popovics

Length 6"   Tied by Winston Moore

KANZ'S MYLAR BAITFISH

Hook: Straight eye, standard length

Wing: A bunch of white FisHair on the top and one on the bottom with several tapering bunches of silver Flashabou (or Mylar) on the sides. On top is a bunch each of long green and blue Ultra Hair or similar

Throat: White FisHair as long as the Ultra Hair

Cheeks: Red hackle barbs, or marabou

Eyes: Hollow plastic

Head: White, painted blue on top to match the top part of the wing

Note: Because of the size and bulk of this fly, materials should be applied in many steps and well cemented.

This is a big fly designed for big fish by Ralph Kanz.

MACK WOOL

Hook: Straight eye, standard length (usually tied about size 7/0 for sailfish)

Wing: White lamb's wool, outside of which are two turquoise and four green rooster tail feathers. The two outermost feathers are painted with a black marking pen as shown

Throat: Rainbow crystal flash over which is white and red lamb's wool

Collar: Light olive lamb's wool

Eyes: Solid plastic or glass

Head: Dark olive lamb's wool

Note: May be fished either with a single or tandem hook.

The Mack Wool is a mackerel imitation that Bob Popovics designed for offshore work. In Costa Rica the sailfish love to eat this one.

MOORE'S BILLFISH BAITFISH

Trailer hook: Turned up eye, short, offset, connected to the front hook by a loop of 65 lb. monofilament, point up

Front hook: Straight eye, standard length

Body: Flat silver Mylar tinsel

Throat: White FisHair

Wing: Green over which is blue FisHair

Head: Red

Note: Variations include dark green over light green to imitate a dorado, and a bright orange exciter pattern

Winston Moore, when we spoke with him in July 1992, had "landed and released 138 Pacific sailfish up to 145 lbs." on flies of this design. He adds an attention-getting, soft foam popper head, dyed red, threaded onto the shock tippet by means of a piece of hollow plastic tubing placed in the soft head.

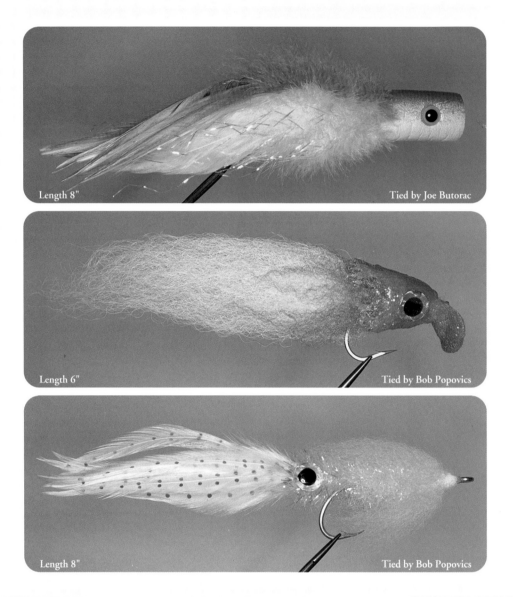

Length 8" Tied by Joe Butorac

Length 6" Tied by Bob Popovics

Length 8" Tied by Bob Popovics

POP-EYE POPPER

Hook: Straight eye, long shank
Tube: Cement a 1" section of flexible tubing over a 1½" section of of hard plastic tubing that will be inserted into the popper head after the fly is done
Wing: Secure to the soft tubing 6 large yellow hackles (fluff and all) on each side, over which are 6 green hackles tied flat on top
Cheeks: Pearl crystal flash on each side, unravelled
Popper head: Soft, closed cell foam painted as shown
Eyes: Solid plastic

Developed in the late 1960's by Joe Butorac of Arlington, Washington.

POP LIPS, BIG FISH

Hook: Straight eye, standard length
Wing: White lamb's wool
Wool head: Red lamb's wool stacked and trimmed to shape including a "bib" of wool in front to form the diving lip
Head and lip: Clear silicone rubber spread over the wool head, shaped as shown and sprinkled with glitter flakes (in order to form the diving lip, work the silicone into the "bib," shape with your fingers, and trim)
Eyes: Peel-off, stick-on prismatic eyes
Note: After applying the eyes and glitter flakes, add a final coat of silicone rubber to the head and lip.

Popovics' Pop Lip flies dart underwater and wiggle like live minnows when retrieved - you have to see them in action to appreciate them.

SHADY LADY SQUID

Hook: Straight eye, long shank
Note: The tentacles, mouth and eyes are tied onto a length of stiff 30 to 50 lb. monofilament that is secured to the hook shank.
Tentacles: About a dozen white hackles speckled with a black marking pen
Eyes: Solid plastic or glass
Mouth: Long fiber pearl crystal chenille wrapped over, around and in front of the eyes
Hook: Straight eye, long shank
Body: Long fiber pearl crystal chenille, veiled with white wool

Bob Popovics of Seaside, New Jersey, ties this squid imitation for offshore fish like tuna and large dolphin.

SELECT BIBLIOGRAPHY

BOOKS

Bates, Joseph D., Jr. 1979. *Streamers & bucktails*. New York: Alfred A. Knopf.

Bay, Kenneth E. 1972. *Salt water flies*. Philadelphia: J.B. Lippincott.

Boyle, Robert H. and Dave Whitlock, ed. 1975. *Fly-tyer's almanac*. New York: Crown Publishers.

_____. 1978. *Second fly-tyer's almanac*. Philadelphia & New York: J.B. Lippincott.

Brooks, Joe. 1968. *Salt water game fishing*. New York: Harper & Row.

Ferguson, Bruce & Les Johnson & Pat Trotter. 1985. *Fly fishing for Pacific salmon*. Portland, Or: Frank Amato Publications.

Kaufmann, Randall. 1992. *Bonefishing with a fly*. Portland, Or: Western Fisherman's Press.

Hanley, Ken. 1991. *California fly tying & fishing guide*. Portland, Or: Frank Amato Publications.

Kreh, Lefty. 1986. *Fly fishing in salt water*. New York: Lyons & Burford.

_____.n.d. (1989). *Salt water fly patterns*. Fullerton, Ca: Maral, Inc.

Leiser, Eric. 1987. *The book of fly patterns*. New York: Alfred A. Knopf.

McClane, A. J., ed. 1965. *McClane's new standard fishing encyclopedia*. New York: Holt, Rinehart and Winston.

Samson, Jack. 1991. *Saltwater fly fishing*. Harrisburg: Stackpole Books.

Tabory, Lou. 1992. *Inshore fly fishing*. New York: Lyons & Burford.

Wentink, Frank. 1991. *Saltwater fly tying*. New York: Lyons & Burford.

PERIODICALS

American Angler. various dates 1990 - 1992. Intervale, NH: Northland Press.

American Angler & Fly Tyer. various dates 1988 - 1990. Intervale, NH: Northland Press.

American Fly Tyer. various dates 1986 - 1987. Intervale, NH: Northland Press.

Fly Fisherman. various dates 1984 - 1992. Harrisburg, Pa: Cowles Magazines.

Fly Fishing Quarterly. various dates 1988 - 1992. Shrewsbury, NJ: Aqua-Field Publishing.

Fly Rod & Reel. various dates 1989 - 1992. Camden, Me: Down East Enterprise.

Fly Tyer. various dates 1978 - 1986. North Conway, NH: Fly Tyer, Inc.

VIDEO

Dennis, Jack. Tying saltwater flies with Jimmy Nix. 1991. Jackson Hole, Wy: Jack Dennis Fly Fishing Video Library.

INDEX TO FLY DRESSINGS

ABOUT THE AUTHORS

Dick Stewart (left) and Farrow Allen

Dick Stewart, has been tying flies since the age of fourteen and has been professionally involved in the fly-fishing industry for almost twenty years. He has authored or co-authored five books including the fly-tying primer *Bass Flies* and the best-selling *Universal Fly Tying Guide*. His saltwater fishing experience began in New Jersey and has since included fly fishing for stripers and bluefish in New England, chasing bonefish and snook in Florida, and offshore casting to sailfish. Formerly editor and publisher of *American Angler* magazine, Dick has settled in the White Mountains area of New Hampshire.

Farrow Allen, moved from New York City to Vermont where for twelve years he owned a fly-fishing shop in the Burlington area. During this time he co-authored a book *Vermont Trout Streams*. A long time fly tier, Farrow has fished extensively for striped bass and bluefish throughout the northeast, and has ventured as far as Costa Rica, fly fishing for sailfish and marlin. He has been associated with *American Angler* magazine and now resides in New Hampshire.

ABOUT THIS BOOK

This is the fourth book in a series of five which cover the majority of recognized fly patterns in use in the United States and Canada. The series is entitled *Fishing Flies of North America* and the individual titles are as follows:

Flies for Atlantic Salmon
Flies for Steelhead
Flies for Bass & Panfish
Flies for Saltwater
Flies for Trout